The Notebook of a Nature-lover

Henry Williamson in 1933 as portrayed by COIA *of the Sunday Referee*

The Notebook of a Nature-lover

Henry Williamson

Illustrations by Michael Loates

The Henry Williamson Society

Collected writings of Henry Williamson previously published by
The Henry Williamson Society:

Contributions to the Weekly Dispatch, 1920–21
Days of Wonder
From a Country Hilltop
Genius of Friendship: T. E. Lawrence
A Breath of Country Air, Parts I & II
Spring Days in Devon
Pen and Plough
Threnos for T. E. Lawrence
Green Fields and Pavements

This collection first published 1996

The Henry Williamson Society
14 Nether Grove
Longstanton
Cambs

Text © The Henry Williamson Literary Estate 1996
Foreword © Loetitia Williamson 1996
Illustrations © Michael Loates 1996

Standard edition ISBN 1 873507 10 0
Limited edition ISBN 1 873507 11 9

All rights reserved. No part of this publication may be reproduced, stored in a retrieval system, or transmitted, in any form or by any means, electronic, mechanical, photocopying, recording or otherwise, without the prior permission of the copyright owners.

Typeset by Cambridge Photosetting Services
Printed and bound in Great Britain

Contents

	page
Foreword	viii

SPRING:

Spring Lures My Husband Away	3
Secret of the Starling's Song	6
When Dawn Breaks over Exmoor	8
The Loneliest Corner of Devon	10
Strange Visitor from the Sea	12
The Romance of a Rail Journey	14
Finding Truth in the Sun's Path	16
Tragedy of the Shot Buzzards	18
A Night in a Farmhouse Kitchen	20
Memories of Twenty Years Ago	22
A Summer Day on the Sands	24
When the Salmon Return	26
The Angler's Paradise	29
Down a Devonshire Lane	31
There was Thunder over Exmoor	33

SUMMER:

Story of a Sticky Business	37
A Storm Idyll	39
My Encounter with a Mother Partridge	41
The Devil's Darning Needle	43
An Exmoor Holiday	45
Some Secrets of my Day's Work	47
The Birds Vanish from their Sanctuary	49
Gulf Stream Brings Strange Visitors to Devon	51
Dawn over Exmoor	53
The Lesson of the Spider	55

	page
AUTUMN:	
Summer Passes	61
Leaping the Weir	63
Bird Migrants of the Stratosphere	65
The Doomed Elm Tree	67
Just a Bridge	69
In Praise of Brighton	71
The Ducks	74
The Sussex Downs	76
Are Animals Trained by Fear?	78
After the Rain	80
WINTER:	
The Dweller on the Hilltop	85
Fisherman's Paradise	87
The Bravest of Birds	89
The Silent Sentinel at the Gate	91
Stark Tragedy in Bird Land	94
The Salmon-leap	96
A Sunday Walk on Exmoor	98
Peal Leaping	100
Out of the Mouth of Babes...	102
Life is Returning to the Moor	104
Hill-top Meditations	106
The Mystery of the Orange Ship	108
Pigeons Come to Breakfast	110
The Country Awakes from its Winter Sleep	112
The Love Song of the Curlew	114
A Message of Hope from the West	116

Editor's Note and Acknowledgements

Henry Williamson began writing his weekly column The Notebook of a Nature-lover for the Sunday Referee in May 1933. It continued, with the occasional gap, until February 1936. During this period Williamson and his family were living in a thatched cottage at Shallowford, near Filleigh in North Devon, and he was in the throes of writing his much-loved classic *Salar the Salmon*, 'every word being chipped from the breastbone', as he was wont to say afterwards. *Salar* was published in October 1935 by Faber and Faber and is in print to this day, a tribute to the remarkable feat of imagination and observation which produced it.

For the Sunday Referee Henry Williamson, his reputation at its zenith, was a prize catch. The caricature by COIA used as a frontispiece was one of a series which included Aldous Huxley, Richard Aldington and Bertrand Russell. The newspaper stated proudly that 'week by week this artist will portray in his own unusual style members of that brilliant team of writers who are building up the Sunday Referee's reputation as the National Newspaper for Thinking Men and Women.'

Many of the earlier Sunday Referee articles were collected and published in *The Linhay on the Downs* (Jonathan Cape, 1934). Clemence Dane wrote of this 'Here is another volume of Henry Williamson's tender, illuminating studies of life in the English countryside.... He knows his fields and woods, understands and perfectly renders back that mingled charm of colour, scent and shape which is the English countryside. He knows, too, how to translate the hidden life of birds and beasts.' The same may well be said of this present anthology, collecting for the first time the remaining Sunday Referee pieces, which recall a Devon that has all but vanished in the sixty years since they were written.

My thanks must go to Ian Rennie, who supplied me with detailed information about Williamson's Sunday Referee contributions; to Mick Loates for his meticulous and delightful line drawings, and especially to Mrs Loetitia Williamson for both her encouragement and her foreword recalling those Shallowford days of so long ago. Unfortunately it has proved impossible to trace the holder of the copyright for COIA's drawing, the use of which is hereby acknowledged. The Henry Williamson Society gratefully acknowledges the permission of the Trustees of the Henry Williamson Literary Estate to publish this collection and to use the salmon colophon from the first edition of *Salar*.

John Gregory

Foreword

by

Mrs Loetitia Williamson

While re-reading these newspaper articles I am taken back in thought to life as it was in the country sixty years ago. So different to life as it is now – then, small children could wander up the lane by themselves to spend their pennies at the village shop, or run through the woods to a cottage half-a-mile away where an old lady made the most delicious ice-cream which she sold in halfpenny and penny cornets, and five and six-year olds could walk the mile-and-a-half to school – so very different now when children are hardly safe in their own gardens.

No electricity in the cottage at Shallowford in those far-off days: oil-lamps and candles; oil cooking stove; coke boiler for hot water; no vacuum cleaner; no electric iron; no washing machine; no fridges or freezers. What a lot we take for granted now. The cottage itself, however, was warm and dry with thick walls and thatched roof. We used to hear the rats running about overhead and through the cob walls and sometimes they would find their way inside, much to the consternation of visitors.

The two neighbouring labourers' cottages were very primitive: cooking was done on an open fire in which whole faggots were burnt. A kettle or cooking-pot would be suspended by a chain over the fire; there must have been an oven of some sort – perhaps a brick oven at the side? The faggots would have been cut by the farm-worker in his own time, and he would be lent a horse and cart from the estate to take them home where they would be built into a tidy stack. This would be their fuel for the whole year. There is no sign of these cottages now. I don't know when they

Foreword

were demolished but the occupants had been moved to more modern dwellings during our time at Shallowford.

One of them, Mrs Ridd, 'Riddy' to the children, was greatly loved. She came and helped in the house at times, and one day when small four-year-old John was 'helping' make pastry, sitting up at the kitchen table, he said 'Be 'ee married to Mr Ridd, Riddy?' Riddy, rather surprised, 'For why, Johnnie?' 'Oh I dunno, I thought perhaps if you wasn't I'd marry you myself one day.' I can see Riddy now, a comfortable warm-hearted Devon woman; no wonder she was a favourite with the children.

I seldom went on the Exmoor walks with Henry, there was too much to do at home; but I do remember one day. We came to a small river and leaning over a bridge we saw a young man fly-fishing. Of course this intrigued Henry – it was after *Salar* was published – and he could not help calling out and giving advice on some technical point. Then he said, 'Have you read a book called *Salar the Salmon*?' 'Of course I have,' replied the man, obviously impatient at having been interrupted. 'I wrote it,' said Henry, 'Good-bye.' I shall never forget the astonishment on the fisherman's face, but by this time Henry was striding away up the hill.

These Exmoor walks were very precious to Henry – but I wonder if there would be the same enchantment now? Then, it was a triumph to find 'Pinkery' pond; now I believe there is a 'proper' path to it. And Dunkery Beacon is no longer as unattainable as it was sixty years ago. Of course there are still wild places and wonderful combes and valleys, but I feel that perhaps members of the Ramblers' Association know them only too well.

There are other changes, too, nearer at hand. The viaduct, over which ran the single line railway track from Taunton to Barnstaple, on which the children, and Henry too, trespassed more than once, is no more. It is now a road-bridge, part of the new by-pass which has shortened by possibly almost two hours the time taken to drive the same distance. No longer do we pass Stag's Head, where the penny ice-creams were made; no longer see the front of Castle Hill, the home of Earl Fortescue – 'The

Lord' as he was known to the villagers who held him in great awe. He was very aware of his duty to his tenants as I found out when returning home from America after some weeks with Henry, who was on a lecture tour in the USA. I was told that 'The Lord' had ridden round several times to the cottage during my absence to make sure that all was well.

Many famous and not-so-famous people came to visit us. I remember C R W Nevinson, the artist, and his wife; Sir Alfred Munnings, and of course C F Tunnicliffe who did the wonderful illustrations for *Tarka* and *Salar*.

It was during these years that Henry did a lot of broadcasting from Bristol, driving there in his Alvis Silver Eagle, and often coming home late at night and weary. It was after one of these occasions on a very dark night, about a mile from home, that he was startled by an owl flying suddenly in front of him, and the car turned over. He, fortunately, was not hurt and the Alvis was repaired. It was eventually restored many years later, and is still running.

Some of the highlights of those days were the visits to Georgeham, to the 'Field' – complete with camping equipment. There was no house there, only Henry's hut and a large garage. The children and I would sleep in the loft of the garage, and Henry would build wonderful bonfires, and we would all go down to the sands to play and bathe.

But eventually Henry became restless for fresh scenes, feeling he had written all he could about the Devon countryside, and so – the migration to the East Coast and a whole new way of life on the Norfolk farm.

Suffolk, 1996

Spring

Spring Lures My Husband Away

By Mrs Henry Williamson

I am writing this article because my husband disappeared this morning – the morning of the 'deadline', the last day of writing the Sunday Referee article for the week.

He said, as he went out: 'I'll be back in half an hour, I'm just going to look at the river'; and, taking his Zeiss monocular glass, he departed.

Now the post is due to go out in an hour's time, it is nearly five o'clock, the two elder boys are just home from school, the baby is shouting 'Goodnight-goodnight-goodnight,' my daughter is asking for her tea, and I am trying to write this.

The Notebook of a Nature-lover

If an author has his trials, they are certainly reflected on an author's wife. Has he had any food today? I don't suppose so. Do I envy his departure? I should say so!

For this is the first real summery day of the year. First of all, we saw a squirrel in the holly tree at the bottom of that part of the garden called the swamp – all that remains of his trout farm. Then we heard the willow wren singing from the honeysuckle bines over the runner, or brooklet, which joins the river a hundred yards away. Then Henry, peering down, noticed the first trout-fry of the season. (He has the most extraordinary sight, and sees too much almost; especially in the house, for his talent cannot be said to extend to domesticity!)

I think it was the sight of that small fish, scarcely longer than a fingernail, that put the wild look in his eye. When I reminded him, as he asked me to, of the article, he gave a furtive sideway glance and muttered something about having to support a dozen parasites, and I knew the stuff about artistic freedom was coming.

So I said, 'Very well, I'll do it, if you do the housework, the mending, the cooking, the beds, see to Baby Robert, and crush the coke for the boiler.'

He appeared not to hear, still staring at the troutling which was wagging enthusiastically at the tail of a miniature pool about six inches square and an inch deep . . . 'I'll be back in half an hour,' he said, vaguely, glancing at the shining azure sky.

That was seven hours ago, and he hasn't returned yet.

It has been a lovely day, the best of the year so far. Gossamers were gleaming upwards soon after breakfast. The air, faintly misty, was a living thing. Midges and other water-flies crossed and floated by the window in scores. We saw a greenfinch disappearing into the top of one of the yew trees on the lawn. A red admiral butterfly, awakened from winter sleep under the thatch, was seen on the aubretias. I took off the clothes of Baby Robert, and let him run about on the lawn, cooing with delight.

As for Henry, he is probably on Exmoor, having followed up

the river to its source, a thing which he has not yet done, but always meant to do.

It makes me happy to think of him for a while as he was before he had all these little mouths to feed, careless and free as the sunshine.

Editor's note: Despite the by-line this was, of course, written by Henry himself. In a recent letter Mrs Loetitia Williamson confirmed that 'Tempting though it is, and much as I should like to, I cannot lay claim to the article . . . it is very Henry-ish, isn't it – all that tiny detail – and all very true!'

Secret of the Starling's Song

Early this morning a starling alighted on the fringe of thatch over my bedroom window and began to pull out reed-motts. This is the thatcher's term for what is loosely called straw. A thatch is not laid with straw, which would soon rot and let in the water, but with unbruised wheaten reed specially selected. A mott is a length of reed.

Well, as this starling was tugging another starling flew beside it, and, bracing its reddish-brown legs, took the mott in its beak and pulled. The newcomer was a female, with plumage slightly less dull. Having thus given his mate a lead, the original starling hopped to a perch over her head and began to sing.

Starlings are mimics, and their songs vary with their locality. If you listen to a London bird, should you be able so to do, you may hear the grate of gears changing, the dull noise of milk bottles being deposited on stone door-steps, the sirens of Thames tugs, and the bark of dogs.

My starling's wings were shivering, his crest was raised, his throat swelled, his beak opened, and he poured his squitchedy din into the misty air of morning. I could not see him; but I knew he was doing it. There it was again, obviously an imitation of a team ploughing.

When I was a boy I put a small wooden box, suitably boarded in except for a small hole, at the top of an elm, and watched a starling tugging off wallflower heads from a garden bed and dropping them into the box. Whenever another starling, female I suppose, flew near he would sing and shake his wings in frenzy of enticement.

My bird had lured a female to my thatch, started a hole, and when a mate came he let her do the work and took to singing, or philosophical musing aloud, or whatever it was, beside her. Possibly his exhortations to her, freely translated, would run like this:

> *The curlew cries sweetly over the green marsh, so can I, much better, listen to this. Ah! but wait, I will now whistle like a train before Filleigh tunnel. How's that? Pretty good, I think. Go on, pull out that mott, my love, the world is lovely today and soon the bacon rind will be flung on the lawn and I'll get you a bit if you work well. Now then, listen to this, doesn't it recall the ploughlands and the worms, the chafer grubs, and those goddam gulls? Wheezy wheedle chikkle me!*

So I imagined the starling thinking, or rather feeling; and with almost a shock I heard it say, in a miniature shout, *Git Bark!*

What further proof was needed? For at every headland in a field, a Devon ploughman shouts to his team, *Get back!*

When Dawn Breaks over Exmoor

A star burned brightly over the tops of the spruce firs where the wild pigeons had not yet awakened. A star? Such a steady shine surely was of a planet. It had not the soft lustre of Venus, which would soon be rising behind my head, in the eastern sky over the distant hills.

I had not looked at a star-map for years. This planet was a stranger.

And yet not a stranger: for during several mornings I had awakened at the end of the night, while the stars were shining and a dark blueness was filtering into the sky, and watched it moving slowly towards the West. If I turned away for a while, closing my eyes and breathing deeply of the cold air stirring to life again – for the airs of night and day are different – the star would be gone, to be found again by moving the head sideways, when it would glitter among the topmost branches of a fir.

It was not yet songlight, but birds were beginning to whisper to one another. A pair of greenfinches which roosted in one of the yews on the lawn below began a low rapid under-twitter, a flow of subtle inflexions, which surely was an inflowing of mutual joy. They nested every year in that tree; either the same pair, or their offspring. For them, as for us, this was the happiest time of the year, and one small bird was expressing to another small bird, the one to the other, their song-talk intertwined, what I was feeling, but in a lesser, duller way.

An owl flew across the window, not seen, but sensed, and a hooting, rattling cry filled the coombe. It was one of those dwarf owls which were introduced into England about eighty years ago, and have since increased a million-fold. They have many cries, not exactly mimics, and not mockers, but between the two. I have heard them wauling like a cat, barking like a dog, wailing like peacocks, and uttering low, sobbing, muffled cries which seemed to be an echo of the snipe's spring 'drumming'.

They are vermin, these little owls, flying by day and by night, and destroying song birds, butterflies, lizards, and even taking fledgelings out of nests.

The star was gone again behind the spruce top. Turning round I saw the sky was an indigo blue flowing to the zenith out of the east. I drowsed, feeling the dawn wind, the least stir of air, on my face. A flute-like sound from the garden, very gentle, and repeated twice, told me that an otter was going back to the river after travelling up the runner which tinkled at the bottom of the garden.

A moment later, it seemed, I opened my eyes and saw a sky of azure, white clouds trailing high in sunshine, rooks noisy, blackbirds, thrushes, and pigeons singing, and the other end of the house filled with bumps and cries of laughter – the children having the early morning rough-and-tumble.

The Loneliest Corner of Devon

The other morning I went to visit someone living in a village which is farther from a railway than any other village in England. My friend was out, and would not be returning until evening, so I went for a walk by myself, following a small stream down the valley to where it fell over the cliffs into the Atlantic.

In summer this runner or brook shrinks to a mere thread. In winter it is only three feet wide and less than a foot deep, but, like its larger brother that falls over the cliff a mile or so southward, it nourishes trout up to three-quarters of a pound in weight – small headed trout, too.

By their small heads one knows that they are fly-feeders, they are not bottom feeders, eating mullheads and smaller trout. They are the fattest trout in Devonshire.

Lifting up a stone in the bed of the rillet, I perceived the reason of their fatness.

On the smooth, dark, algae-covered part of the stone, which was touched by water, several small nymphs of the blue dun were wriggling; and on the lower part of the stone which had been embedded in clay were no fewer than seven yellowish-white grubs, with brown heads, each concealed in a sort of muddy silken sack tacked to the stone.

Were these grubs of the mayfly, I wondered? They looked like those grubs which bore into the bark of spruce trees, except that they were more lively and slightly thinner.

I wandered down the valley of rough grazing and storm-sheared trees towards the edge of the land. The stream fell from the slanting crevice in a pool and from the pool it leapt and bubbled on the boulders of the shore.

I slid down the rocky sheer and sat beside the pool. The shore was strewn with great pieces of rock which the Atlantic storms had broken from the cliffs.

Some of the rocks would be ground smooth by the tides and rolled along the base of the promontory until washed up on the beach of Westward Ho! perhaps in the twenty-second century A.D. There are pools on this wild shore where conger eels and lobsters move; black and sodden timbers of ships lie there under the weed; gulls cry their cadaver-cries overhead. There was a strange feeling of aloneness on this inhuman coast.

I went up a cliff-path and climbed towards the sun. There is a footpath, continuous except for towns and where it has been widened into roads, around the entire island which is called Great Britain. This particular section of it led on south into Cornwall.

I came to another valley, where the larger stream fell over a break in the cliff to its pool in the rock below. At my approach a heron flew away up the valley.

Next week I hope to tell you of a remarkable sight I witnessed while sitting beside that waterfall.

Strange Visitor from the Sea

White tresses of water were being blown back over the edge of the cliff by the strong Atlantic wind. I was sitting on a rock, by the cliff gap, where the stream fell over to the shore below. The water fell sheer for ten feet or more.

While I was staring at the white, rough pillar of water, ever changing and yet always remaining the same, I saw to my astonishment what had probably been the cause of interest to the heron, which had flown up at my arrival – a sea-trout about fifteen inches long leapt out of the turbulence below and began to swim up the waterfall.

I saw spots along the thickness of the back, an instant before the fish, quivering with sea-power, *pierced* the water and remained there, dim and blurred in shape, slowly ascending the fall. It vibrated within the glassy pillar up which it moved slowly.

It was the most remarkable fish jump or manœuvre that I have ever had the good luck to see. The sea-trout had come out of the turmoil as if shot by a catapult for quite four feet. I could almost hear its power *thrumming* into the rough roar of the water. (Salmon accelerating suddenly in a slow-flowing pool make a drumming noise clearly audible by the human ear; akin to the noise made by cock-snipe during the nesting season.)

It had actually ascended, inch by inch, for fully a yard, before it fell back exhausted and was washed away. It seemed impossible that any fish would ever get up that fall, which was nine or ten feet high.

I had never heard or read of peal, which is the West Country name for sea-trout, being caught in the stream I was watching; possibly the peal I saw was a stray fish which had come up with the tide, and was excited by the high oxygen content of the fresh water.

What fun it would be, I thought, staring at the water, to own or lease this stream, and to build a series of diminishing dams below the fall and then make some hatchery boxes and start with a few eyed ova, say a hundred thousand, of sea-trout.

The fry would swim out of the grills, and perhaps five thousand would live to grow into fish six inches long after two years, when they would lose their brown trout coat and red spots, and become silvery, and drop down into the sea. After wandering round the west coast of England and perhaps Ireland for one or two years, several might find their way back, ascend the pass between the rocks, and spawn in the stream, thus founding a new branch of the great sea-trout family – for sea-trout and salmon, like swallows and cuckoos, return to their native places.

I waited half an hour, until I was as cold as the rock on which I sat, but I did not see the little water-traveller again.

The Romance of a Rail Journey

It was daughter Margaret's fifth birthday, and for her 'treat' I took the children to Lynton for the day on the dwarf railway from Barnstaple.

The railway may soon be closed, and a journey on it is an adventure.

Margaret, John, Windles, his friend 'Slee boy', and I stood on the platform at the beginning of our journey and inspected the miniature engine.

'Cor, look at the high funnel,' said John.

'I say, there's a cow-catcher, but I suppose it's for the red deer, and what a huge dome – I bet it takes the driver a long time to polish it every morning,' said Windles, whose job it is every Saturday to shine the brass door handles at home.

We climbed into one of the little carriages, the whistle blew a high comic note, and by the noise we were soon travelling at a great rate. Only the countryside seemed to be passing very slowly.

'Cor, she's getting up steam,' said John, as we stood at Snapper Halt a few minutes later.

'She may burst,' I told him. (The engine was wreathed in white.) 'But perhaps the driver's only stoking her up for a cup of tea.'

'Don't talk rot, dad,' scoffed Windles; then, seeing my face, 'Is it true?'

'Probably not. But I remember the driver of the French troop train which took us up the line to St. Omer in 1914 giving us water to make tea with in our mess tins.'

The train followed the deep wooded valley of the River Yeo, on the upgrade all the way. The valiant little engine hauled us fussily through hail and rain; then the fields were green again, but everywhere streaming with water.

Between Chelfham (pronounced Chillum) and Parracombe (pronounced Parrakmb) we stopped abruptly. Driver and fireman alighted and walked forward. Heads peered out of windows. The driver returned with a lamb under his arm. The lamb was put over the wire fence, restored to its frantic ewe.

Just before slowing up for Lynton the rain began to fall heavily, and we were glad of our raincoats, brought reluctantly by the children and bundled on the wooden rack over our heads.

We walked down the steep, stony track to Lynmouth, and, after some ginger-beer at an inn at the foot of Sinai Hill, we ate our sandwiches in the shelter of a baker's porch, while the rain lashed down. After a three hours' exploration of the beach in the rain, we took the funicular carriage up the cliff to Lynton, and climbed to the station again.

Perhaps it was the children's first and last journey on that little railroad, for it is probably to be discontinued at the end of the coming summer. Lynton and Lynmouth sent a delegation to the Southern Railway representatives in Barnstaple recently to urge its continuance; and all but one of the delegates travelled there by motor-car.

Editor's note: In his recent book *Discovering Britain's Lost Railways* (Automobile Assoc., 1995) Paul Atterbury declared that 'For citizens of Barnstaple, the only railway they really considered their own was the narrow gauge Lynton & Barnstaple. Sponsored by the publisher Sir George Newnes and opened in 1898, this little railway, with its 1 ft 11 in gauge and its smart locomotives and carriages, always aroused strong local support even if it never made much money . . . Subject from the 1920s to increasing competition from road traffic, especially motor coaches, it finally gave up the struggle and closed in 1935 . . .'

Finding Truth in the Sun's Path

The road runs under a hill almost direct to Tavistock. If you want to avoid motor-cars and towns there is a turning to the left that leads slowly downhill to the valley of the Burn, which can be crossed near the little railway station of Mary Tavy.

You will be in a country of mines and chimneys, most of them derelict amidst grey heaps of deads, which have been piled up from the shafts. On some of them not even a thistle grows, for they are the refuse of the arsenic mines.

The main road from Okehampton to Tavistock and Plymouth runs through Mary Tavy, but the mines are in the valley beyond. A mile away lies the brother village of Peter Tavy, with the high ground of the tors rising into the sky.

In spring it is a good walk to follow the road out of the north end of Peter Tavy by the church, and walk for a couple of miles above the river, until the lane forks. Take the left fork and follow up the river, along the tracks of sheep and cattle. After awhile you will pass a hut circle and come to Tavy Cleave, which is a wild and rocky place, with the hills going up on either side strewn with immense blocks of granite.

In spring herons build their nests near here, on tops of stunted trees no higher than a man.

The river flows brown but clear over pink and black rocks, some of which must weigh thousands of tons and which are almost as flat as billiard tables. Beside the river are many good grassy places for pitching a small tent; and you must bathe naked in a pool as the sun comes up in the morning to feel yourself living as God made you.

It is always best to travel into the unknown, and from Tavy Cleave you should follow the water up past its junction with the

Finding Truth in the Sun's Path

Rattlebrook, and either climb the 1,850 feet height at Tavy Head and across Cut Hill, which is nearly 2,000 feet high; or continuing up the valley for half a mile, turn right-handed at the next water junction and walk between Fir Tor and Little Kneeset, and so to Cut Hill.

Many otters have come this way before you, as you will see if you are observant.

Two miles away to the north is Cranmere. From Cut Hill, on a spring day, one surveys the world with grand feelings. If you rest there, lying on your back, your face held to the sun and your eyes closed, you will learn that the Truth for which philosophers seek is only an emanation of their own character and environment.

Never try and isolate Truth from the true sun.

Tragedy of the Shot Buzzards

At the top of the hill we sat down and rested, watching five buzzards soaring above us over Silkwood Top. The birds circled in tiers, one above the other, and their cries came clearly to us, melancholy drooping whistles from the height of the sky.

There used to be a fire-guard in my cottage made out of the heads, wings, and feet of three buzzards, which were shot in Spreacombe Woods during the first winter of my writing career. Some fool had shot them casually while waiting for pigeons in the pine-wood; he had walked off home and left the wounded birds lying at the base of one of the tall pines.

There I found them, having returned from the village in the dark when someone told me three hawks had been shot and left to die there. A flapping of wings and a noise of wheezy breathing in the winter night led me to where, in the light of a match, I saw them lying.

I killed them. They were heavy to carry back to the Higher House Inn where in those days I had meals, and I remember laying them on the long table in the bar and measuring the spread of wings, being disappointed that it was only forty-four inches.

The three buzzards were taken to the taxidermist in Barum, and made into a large fire-shield, although what was needed in that old cottage was not so much a fire-shield as a draught-stopper.

The shield never pleased me; and I grew tired of explaining to visitors that I had not shot the birds. And after the hen next door had got used to my habit of scaring her with it, and the dog in Hole Farm no longer barked when he saw the staring yellow eyes and curved beaks approaching, there was nothing more to be got out of it.

So I gave it to my neighbour's child Ernie, who, when he had scared into indifference all the hens and cats and dogs in the village, took it to Sunday School, where the parson's voice ordered him to take the barbaric thing away.

The last I saw of it was lying on my neighbour's rubbish heap, 'ratting' (rotting) down for top-dressing. There was a little arsenic on the skins, to keep away moths, just enough, if it got on a potato or a cabbage, to act as a tonic to the family.

One needed a tonic occasionally, living in those damp and dark cottages below the churchyard.

A Night in a Farmhouse Kitchen

Barking dogs greeted us in the farmyard, and the farmer's wife agreed to let us have three bedrooms for a shilling each the night.

Starlings running to feed among the lush grass of the sloping field seen through the kitchen window were not more hungry or eager than we were, sitting at the long table with its candle burns and cuts of saw and knife, and its oaken stretchers worn concave by the feet of three centuries, the floor of chilly stone spread with the hides of deer shot and snared in the woods around the farm.

Big cups of tea; grey-brown farmhouse bread and salted butter; clome basin of scald cream with crisp yellow crust; eggs, lettuces, radishes, honey, more tea, and cheese with saffron cake.

We sat round the hearth, or, rather, in the hearth, which was eight feet wide and six feet deep, and made of slate slabs laid edge upwards, so that the heat spread out and was held in depth all the winter.

We sat and rested, happy and content, our ease earned by our bodies after the long walk.

A bench stood on short legs each side of the hearth, one carved with the outline of a bullock, the other of a stag with all its rights – each beam or antler bearing brow, bay, and tray, and three points on top – 'three p'n tap,' as they said in that kitchen.

One of the sons of the house was listening with headphones to an old 1923 wireless set on a side-table waiting for the county cricket scores, and afterwards for dance music.

I made notes of the hearth, its engines and utensils, which were:

(a) Two lapping crooks, hanging from the chimney bar, one supporting a five-gallon kettle, the other a cauldron.

A Night in a Farmhouse Kitchen

(b) A handymaid, or cranked length of iron, with a brass handle knob fixed to the handle of the kettle. This acted as lever when hot water was wanted, and also saved the hand being burned.

(c) A tripod.

(d) A cast-iron frying-pan 18in. in diameter, and weighing 14lb.

(e) Two fire-dogs or irons, their bosses or facings dull-bright with constant hand-touches.

(f) Two clome ovens for baking bread, one on either side of the hearth, both black-leaded and shining. Bread was baked twice a week; a fire of furze or thorn – woods which burn readily and give the best heat – kindled and fed in each egg-shaped oven, and left until the embers begin to dim and breathe with ash – when they are raked out, the oven dusted with a malkin – bundle of rags on a stick – the dough placed inside, and the door shut.

'Butiful plumm' bread is baked this way, bread which seems never to become stale or leathery.

Memories of Twenty Years Ago

It was too late that afternoon to attempt to reach Cranmere, the boggy hill in the middle of Dartmoor, where five rivers have their source, so we decided to walk to the moorland village of Belstone, to find accommodation for the night.

We found it in a farmhouse where there was a very fat tame pig, who was sleeping, with a kitten and half-blind old dog, in the kitchen armchair when we arrived. And there he remained most of the time we were there, merely grunting when we tried to shift him.

The next morning, after a breakfast of ducks' eggs and very fat bacon – leading one to think that the pig's predecessor had spent most of its time in the armchair – we set off along the track leading up to the hillside of the Taw Valley. Before us curlew and snipe flew up from their feeding. Clear and fast among its mossy boulders hastened the little river, broadening where cattle and wild ponies had trodden bays of broken granite gravel.

Walking beside the river meant water in our boots, so we climbed the peat hags and up the side of the hill, coming to a dry wall of granite called Irishman's Wall.

A female sparrow-hawk flew up from a tumulus, its plucking place. There lay the remains of her kill, the broken skull and long beak of a snipe, its wings, feathers, and gizzard. The tumulus was also visited by a fox; several pellets of greyish fur and broken rabbit bones lay near it. Perhaps the fox at night came for what the sparrow-hawk left by day.

The hillside rose steeper, and so we returned to the river. While we were walking here we heard a dull, faraway report, succeeded by a swishing noise, and, with a loud plop, a dud shell fell fifty yards away. We remembered that this part of the moor was an artillery range, and we were under the arc of fire. As we walked we heard behind us the familiar chromatic whines of heavy stuff, and near the summit of a Tor on our left front there appeared the fan-shaped bursts of high explosive shells. *Womp-womp-womp-womp.*

It was a strange sensation, that of being two personalities at the same time. One thought now that if the War came again one would have no apprehension about death. It is only the very young who long for immortality.

With a mild shock one realised that over twenty years ago the British Expeditionary Force was falling back in exhaustion before the right wing of von Kluck's army-group, and we were awaiting orders to go overseas.

It seemed but yesterday that one was marching through the Surrey countryside, while villagers and farmers came out with baskets of fruit and jugs of milk and beer for the brigade. How hot was that August sun, how heavy our equipment, how sore our feet, how proud we were afterwards that not a man of the battalion fell out. How we longed for that burning sun three months later, standing all day and all night in the flooded trenches of Ypres.

Now the whining of the shells almost drew the heart out of the breast for those vanished scenes and faces. Then I was thinking how good it was to be alive and free on the wild moor, life clear and natural as the water running on the rock all around us.

A Summer Day on the Sands

To where I was lying naked and natural among pebbles and dry tide-wrack floated several miles of wave-sounds. My hands grasped hot, loose sand, which slipped through my idle fingers.

Turning my head sideways I saw a low, blue horizon quivering over the sands. The mirage dissolved while I was raising myself on my elbow, and small specks in which movement was just visible became clear again.

Lowering my head to the sand level, I saw the specks melt and crumble and disappear into the mirage once more.

The people were about a mile and a half distant. In another half-hour I should have to recivilise myself: to put on my trousers.

My senses were nearly absorbed by the sun; my body was buoyant on the white sandy shore of this shallow coast. I was empty of self-life as the blue butterflies flickering over the scentless flowers of sea-rocket, idly attracted by living colour in the desert of sand.

Summer sea and azure air and blue butterflies were flecks of sky. My body was relaxed and warm in the sun, my mind empty of self-thoughts.

A white gull was oaring itself serenely through the blue above me; a lark was a singing speck over the marram grasses yellow-fringing the sky.

Along the line of pale brown and azure pebbles below the hot, loose sand a ring-plover was stalking gravely, sometimes bowing its head as though to pick up food.

But its thoughts were not of food, for near me its young were crouching, and when the anxiety of the bird was too heavy it freed the heaviness from its breast with a low, fluting cry as of pain.

Hearing this, I moved away, and lay on my back again and tried to empty myself of thought, to lie relaxed and warm in the sun. But memory was alive with its wraiths and shadows, and it seemed sad that the life I had known on these very sands was gone for evermore from the sunshine.

For here I had sat in past summers with a friend, now dead, and we had talked of many things, and in his presence the world had seemed as beautiful as imagination would have it be. For God was in that man, whom the world called Lawrence of Arabia.

Editor's note: T E Lawrence died on 19 May 1935 following a motorcycle accident six days earlier. The above was written less than a fortnight afterwards. Henry Williamson gave a full account of his friendship with Lawrence in *Genius of Friendship* (Faber, 1941) and *Threnos for T E Lawrence* (The Henry Williamson Society, 1994).

When the Salmon Return

Between Dartmouth in Devon and Start Point, a distance of about a dozen miles as the raven flies when returning to its carrion feast, there lies a shingle bank between the sea and the road.

To the hiker who may have come from the red cliffs of Sidmouth, or from the great ironstone crags of the northern coast, this low gravelly coast is an unusual sight. There is a lake just beyond the road; but I will tell you about that another time.

This is about the sea, and that beautiful fish, the salmon.

At a place called Hallsands, where the sea has ruined the old village, I observed a method of taking these fish, which was new, and therefore intensely interesting to me.

At a vantage point on the cliffs above an old man was standing by a small hut made of driftwood and corrugated iron. He might have been seventy years old. He bid me good morning, while continuing to peer down into water two hundred feet below. To my eyes the water on the shingle was clear for about six feet only from the shore. Some distance away a small boat, a net piled in its stern, with oars shipped, lay on the beach.

Suddenly, as I peered with him, the old fellow bent his back and stared intently in the direction of some dark submerged rocks. I could see nothing except the sea. 'There they be,' he said, pointing a crooked finger. 'The trouble is they'm going the wrong way.' He stared like a cat. 'Ah, they'm turning now.' He shouted, and, taking off his cap, pointed at the rocks. Still I could see nothing. 'Ten pounds' worth of fish,' he muttered.

Men appeared out of the ruins of the old village; they ran over the shingle; the boat was launched; the net was shaken over the stern while the two men rowed vigorously in an arc towards where the watcher was pointing. As I stared, disappointed in my poor sight, a slim shape curved out of the water not six feet from the shore, and sank into its bubbled plunge.

The widening surge of the ripples had hardly settled when the salmon leapt again about twenty yards farther on. Then I could see a shadow-shape moving in the dim greenish water.

The fish, after their two years of feeding in the deep Atlantic, were travelling in shallow water along the coast, seeking the estuary of the River Dart.

I ran down the path, and so to the shore. The seine of the net was drawn nearer. Had they missed the school of ten or a dozen salmon? The last of the net came in rapidly. Ah! One fish only.

It threshed the net in vain. A hand gripped it by the tail, it was carried up the shingle and dropped in a small hollow. There it writhed and writhed, seeking escape from the terrible elements of air and sunlight. It was small-mouthed, silver-frosty, scarcely spotted – a maiden fish.

How many thousands of sea miles had it travelled since, two years previously, it had dropped down to the sea from one of the Dartmoor brooks, a little six-inch red-spotted parr, looking like a trout? So it had grown and dreamed of returning; now it was flapping on the shingle, trying with the last of its life to find what it had lost.

I wanted to crack it on the head with my stick, as fresh-caught salmon are stunned in the Taw and Torridge estuary where I live; but that would be interference with the property of others.

Climbing the cliff again, I sat awhile beside the old man, a very gentle, nice old fellow. He told me that the usual cruising speed of the salmon along that coast was about six miles an hour; that it could swim for short distances, in terrific acceleration, at about twenty.

While we talked his vigilance never ceased. Again he arose, pointing; I saw nothing; ah yes! a bluish-white flicker under the dull blue water. He shouted, and held out his hat. The boat put out. The net was dropping at about half its arc when a series of waves was torn on the water; the fish had turned, and were gone over the rocks. Philosophically the boat returned; the net was shaken out and repiled; the watcher relaxed and sat on his chair, and I went happily on my journey.

The Angler's Paradise

I had heard of a long brackish lake lying behind a raised beach of shingle, along the south coast of Devon, the haunt of wild fowl and small reed birds, the habitation of droves of rudd and perch; and of pike, those sharks of fresh water with the immobility and dash of alligators, which nourish themselves on the fish therein, and were in incredible numbers.

As I passed through the village of Strete signs of the proximity of Slapton Ley were in the fences made of long slender reed-like miniature bamboo poles, keeping sea-wind and vulgar gaze from garden and window.

I left the main road and took a short, direct cut down to the low prospect of shingle beach becoming discernible in the mist below. This mist was blown away as I came to the sea almost level with the yellow shingle, but the wet west wind told of more rain to come. I walked on the sward beside the road, a relief to the feet. On my left hand was the sea; on my right hand was the reedy mere.

The water, almost concealed by tall, yellowish reeds of the past summer, made plainer the chit-chittering of reed buntings, the brittle excited song of the sedge warbler, the melancholy croak of the water-hen, the sharper cries of coots and grebes. Wild duck hurtled under the grey clouds.

After a mile there appeared a building or cluster of buildings roofed with thatch and tarred corrugated iron. It bore the somewhat surprising name of the Royal Sands Hotel.

When I entered, the mental picture of its interior, given by the northern approach to this place, was immediately changed. Fishing hats and fishing rod cases were in the lobby; pewter and brass shone against old furniture; the bar, small and snug, was warmed by a tiny Victorian fireplace. Round the walls were stuffed specimens of pike, roach, rudd, and a great silver eel weighing about six pounds.

In the bar I talked with two sportsmen from Birmingham. One of them had fished all over the world, and we exchanged reminiscences of brook trout in Canada. His companion begged me to look at the Record Book before I left, wherein were particulars of amazing baskets. Twenty or thirty pike weighing between four and twenty pounds each was quite a usual daily catch by one rod. It was the usual practice to put the pike back, having weighed them.

As for the red-finned rudd, and the black-barred perch, the trouble with these would appear to be the impossibility of getting enough worms and maggots in the district. More fish than bait!

If you set out with, say, 10,000 maggots, you found that this only sufficed for the first hour: and for every maggot you had you got two fish: and for every fish you got you saw a thousand more: and for every fish you saw there were a million hidden in the Ley.

Indeed, the waters at times of spawning appeared to be rising up and shifting themselves about several acres at a time. Fishermen invariably exaggerate – nature's way of restoring the awful vacuum caused by the difference between dream and reality, but here I certainly got the impression that reality exceeded any dream.

And all because of lime-stone, which formed snails and shrimps, which made the fishes numerous and fat, which nourished the pike, which – and so on, down to the fishing tackle trade.

Down a Devonshire Lane

It is a stereotypic lament of some English people that dialect and regional mannerisms of speech will shortly vanish, and we shall all speak like BBC announcers.

Meanwhile the local speech goes merrily on, unaffected by the restraint and impartiality of Broadcasting House.

Last night, for instance, I overheard the following, from one farmer standing in a sunken lane to another on the hedge above.

'Aiy,' the one with bramble-torn cap and coat and breeches was saying, 'there be lots of bliddy rats about the viels now. Hundreds and thousands of the bliddy things. Why, t'other night I stood by the gate upalong, and if one rat rinned over me boots, why, I tell 'ee, midear, there was thousands! I kep still, I had me gun, too, I could have shute a score with each barrel, but I knew if I so much as kecked one of the beggars with me boot, t'others would have mobilised me.

'I'll tell 'ee, the Government should do something 'bout rats. Them'n all for taking your money, but what about ridding us of rats? Last winter I took ninety-three of the beggars one morning out of my gins tilled in one viel. Ninety-three! Then there was thousands of the critturs left in the rabbuts' buries. Aiy, thousands and thousands!

'Cordarn, I caught one and tarred it, a girt stag-rat, and I let'n go agen, hoping he'd drave the others. But still I couldn't keep no eggs or bliddy chickens or chicken food, they ate the bliddy lot. Fast as I'd trap a couple of hundred, they'd spring up agen.

'One night, I'll tell 'ee, midear, I hear'd a great galloping about on the ceiling over me aid (head), and my missus zaid to me, "It be like a cart and hoss passing overaid, whatever can it be, Jack?" I zaid, "Tes they rats up auver." I coulden get a wink of slape all night, back and 'vore the beggars was proper galloping, like a aerial durby it was up there. Aiy. I tilled a gin for the beggars, but couden catch nought.

'One day, tho', I cornered one behind the cupboard, and a bliddy girt stag-rat 'twas, jimmering and chammering at me, clinging to the bliddy wall, just out of reach of my stick it was, and wan bliddy cat on the top of the bliddy cupboard, anither on the shelf, and a couple of dogs waiting below. I kept the beggar pressed there agen the bliddy wall with me stick. I warn't going vor leave'n now I'd got'n, not if I stayed there all night, and the cats and dogs biding there too. Missus fetched a long stick but the bliddy thing was bent, and wouldn't titch the stag-rat, which opened its mouth and showed its teeth to me.

'Jimmering and chammering it was, with the cats howling up above and the dogs a-roaring and a-bawling down below and me yelling at the missus to yett (heat) the poker in the vire, I'd burn the beggar out of it if it wouldn't come out, cruelty or no cruelty.

'Of course I knowed if one of they inspectors for the abolition of cruelty in hanimals was to have comed along, I should have been into Town, but what about cruelty of the bliddy rats to me, unable to get a wink of slape with them tritting 'bout overhead like a hossrace.

'So missus yett up th' poker, and I pressed 'n into the bliddy rat, saying burn, you beggar, burn, and cordarn, the bliddy withering thing burst into vlames and rinned down the wall and not a bliddy dog would titch it.

'Lucky the door was shut, else 'twould have rinned out and maybe set vire to me neighbour's ricks, for 'twas the self-same bliddy rat I had tarred. I s'pose the ither bliddy rats had drove 'n, because of the smell, and th' beggar had comed into my place.

'I tell 'ee, there's hundreds and thousands of bliddy rats in the viels today.'

The ragged cap was lifted, and the shaggy scalp scraped by broken nails.

Then the conversation or monologue continued in the same language, the farmer telling the identical story again, word for word, laugh for laugh, in the traditional Devon manner.

There was Thunder over Exmoor

Horseflies were troublesome in the hot still air beside the river. How often in the past had I longed for a sudden thunderstorm while fishing here beside the alders and oaks, my horsehair cast and small hackled fly entangled in some spray or bramble, and a sudden stab in cheek or neck telling me that one of the grey-speckled brutes, flying so silently, had settled there and driven its artesian well through the layers of my skin.

A thunderstorm that would damp the wings of the horseflies, especially those with green and red heads, and beat them into the water, where the trout would take them with those suck-snapping noises so exciting to a fly-fisherman on a moorland stream.

It was thundery weather today, with forked flashes splitting the darkness over Exmoor, but no rain down here. The trout had ceased to rise, and I sat on a bank of gravel and did nothing but idly watch the water. The hot deadness of the air before the first flashes and the release of rain appeared to press on the water, and the fish were on the bottom, scarcely moving, as they lie during a frost.

Trout are sensitive as water to the varying pressure of the atmosphere. But the life most affected is that of the ephemeridæ, or nymphs which await the final moment of their water-life before swimming up at noon and changing into flies of such beauty and delicacy that they must, in emotion of their brief aerial life before dying at sunset, experience more rapture and loveliness than is in the music of Wagner or Delius.

One is so often asked, What is the so-called mystery of trout rising, and then going off the feed suddenly, and, as many anglers seem to think, mysteriously? The 'mystery' is food. These trout –

unlike the chalk-stream trout, which have an abundance of food – are always ready to eat.

When the flies are hatching, they move into the best positions in the runs to take the nymphs. And the nymphs hatch – Olive Duns, Yellow Sallies, Pale Wateries, Stone Flies – usually about noon, when the weather is light and warm.

Hence the noonday rise of trout.

When there is food, the trout get it; and when there is none, as before thunder or in frost or cold spells of north-east or north-west wind, the trout remain quiescent, as I am at this moment, lying peacefully on the gravel bank and rather hoping to see a wall of storm water rushing down the river.

But in this country such a thing happens only once in a lifetime.

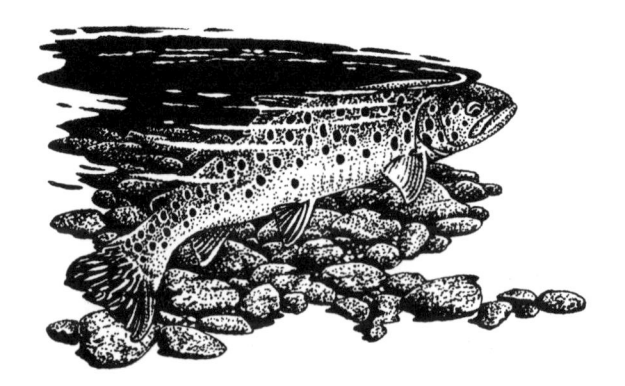

Summer

Story of a Sticky Business

This is Cranmere, which I refuse, pot-boiling writer though I be, but no imitator, to describe as the Mecca of Dartmoor pilgrims. Neither shall I describe it as a dump of orange peel and other litter, including bottles and ourselves. We came to Cranmere after prolonged goat-like hoppings from peat hag to peat hag, linked and arising out of the brown bog.

I had forgotten the exact location of Cranmere, so we went round and round in ignorant circles until we saw a figure, accompanied by a dog, walking rapidly up the slope from another direction. We went towards him, and our goat-like hoppings ceased when we realised that the stranger was walking on the brown patches of bog, into which his boots pressed firmly to the welts only. We followed him here.

Far away beyond Great Mis Tor and Maiden Hill lying to the south, a mist, or cloud, or fog, seemed to be rising unevenly, and I felt glad that my Service prismatic compass was in my pocket. The wind had dropped, the sky was overcast, and visibility seemed to be growing less.

There's a story of a man shooting snipe just about here, who seeing a hat on the ground absentmindedly gave it a kick. A voice came from under the hat, saying 'What be kickin' me 'at vor, you?'

'Aw, be theer a mun under thaccy 'at?'

''Ess, and 'oss under 'ee, too.'

The sportsman inquired what the hat was doing there, and the voice under it said, 'Feyther was upalong looking vor sheep with Billy Budd, but Billy Budd came rinning back to the varm, saying "Varmer be vallen into th' moire; do 'ee come quick and pull'n out, or er'll be a-go."'

"'Aw, Billy, 'ow var be 'er vallen in, tho'?'

"'Er be right in up to 'er ankles, 'er can't get out.'

"'Er can't get out, Billy, did 'ee zay, surenuff?'

"'Ess fay.'

"'Aw Billy, so 'er be right in up to 'er ankles, tho! If 'er be vallen in up to 'er ankles, Billy, 'er can get out, surely?'

'Naw, 'er can't, I tell 'ee, 'er'll be a-go.'

'Which way be 'er vallen in, tho'?'

"'Er be vallen in 'ade virst.'

'So us both jumped on th' ould 'oss an' yurr us be, looking for feyther.'

With that the hat disappeared in the mire and the sportsman continued his interrupted search for snipe.

A Storm Idyll

While thunder was rolling from cloud to cloud the river shone with a white greyness. The green of pasture and oak leaves had an extraordinary stillness, as though the valley light were under water light. Nothing was happening in air or earth or water; life was waiting, stagnant, while the heat lifted in bourdons of sound that travelled leagues, and returned to meet new shocks from the slate quarries of the summer sky.

I realised that I was part of the suspended life. I stood at the edge of the run, at the edge of the fast water running into the pool. My two-ounce rod lay on the grass. The fly-box was open in my hand. There was no energy to select another fly. Nor was there reason; nothing stirred. For half an hour I had been moving upstream, throwing a hackled fly into all likely places. That was all.

Whiter and whiter the river had gleamed as though it were oil moving there. The eyes were hurt by it. Even the horseflies, which during the past two days of sub-tropical heat had risen in thousands, were gone. Heavy-winged and burring, they had flown to rest on alder leaf and bramble.

Then I heard a cry. I was wrong; there was movement somewhere.

A quarter of a mile upriver two small white figures were running on the bank. I had forgotten the children bathing under the waterfall. Rod in hand, I waded across the gliding shallow and came to them.

It was now greenly dark. Violet flashes ran down the clouds above the lower slopes of the moor. A pheasant grated wildly in the tenebrous spruce plantations on the hillside. A young sheepdog appeared along the cart track through the park, fleeing silent and fast, pursued by something we could not see.

The children skipped about in and out of the water, enjoying some game of their own. The boy picked up an old brass candlestick lying on the gravel and held it high, laughing at his thought of a candlestick in the water. That candlestick appeared to be alight; the air crackled; colossal noise fell greyly; the white figures were blurred. Everywhere glassy toadstools grew on the river.

Cries of terror came from the children. They were getting wet in the rain! Oh, oh, where were their clothes! In the house! O! O! Cries of despair and misery.

'Quick, quick, daddy. Can't you see we are getting wet?'

No argument or exhortation consoled them. Hadn't they been wet before? What was the difference between one wet and another? Weren't the large raindrops quite warm, much warmer than the river?

No use. It was raining, and they would get wet. They howled, gibbering with rage because I would not share their plaint.

At last I threw off coat and trousers, and went into the river. It was a strange feeling, swimming with multitudinous pillars of water arising level with one's eyes, millions of ice-flowers growing instantly and blossoming with white water-drops spilling.

Never have I seen rain, or such yelling children. Would they come in? No, they ran home, weeping, because they were naked in the storm: because it hadn't happened before.

Isn't that the history of all mankind?

My Encounter with a Mother Partridge

In Devon they say at cottage doors that all kittens born in May should be drowned at birth. 'Nasty li'l toads, they be; they'll fetch znakes into the place.'

Yesterday, coming home from tennis at a house a dozen miles away, I stopped at a post-office in a hamlet and there, under the little red pillar box in the wall, lay (a) four vipers, (b) one grass snake, (c) two slow-worms. All dead.

Seeing me turn them over gingerly with my canvas-rubber shoe, a small-headed black cat jumped lightly down from the wall, chirruped a greeting, rubbed herself against my leg, and then started gently to play with an adder three feet long. She had bitten it across the neck.

'Proper li'l dear for znakes, her be,' said the postmistress. 'Her ban't afraid of them, noomye! Her'll catch 'em for a pastime! 'Twas a May cat, you know; all other cats be afraid to titch 'em!'

Curious; one lives and learns. Hitherto I had thought the saying to be meaningless.

Another picture. Walking in a field where many small trees are growing, I saw suddenly, less than six inches from my right foot, two partridges squatting on the ground, in the shadow of a *pinus insignis* two feet high. I stood still, daring only to blink my eyes. At the least movement they would fly away. Were they two hens, each on a nest?

Then a horsefly stung my leg (I was wearing only a pair of shorts), and I started. They flew up with loud grating cries, and a shower of diminutive partridge chicks fell from under their wings. One of the old birds, the mother, fell again half a dozen yards away, and began to run through the long grass, uttering cries of distress and trailing a wing apparently broken. The chicks, speckled and dabbled in shades of brown and yellow, clambered laboriously over the grasses, and soon their cheeping ceased.

Meanwhile I moved away, going backwards to avoid treading on any chick. The mother bird followed me, and then retreated as I went round in a semi-circle towards my hut in the far corner of the field. Near the hedge bank she flew up, making a loud noise of wings, as though she were a clockwork bird with wooden pinions, and dropped on the top of the hedge.

Not wishing to distress her even for the sake of science (or cash) I walked away rapidly, and she flopped down and followed me through the grass. I ran, and she actually pursued me, half flying, half running through the long grass.

This was unfair, I thought; so I stopped, and whistled like a curlew, a cry familiar to her, I thought.

Whether a recognition of the whistle as non-hostile, or whether the distance between me and her chicks reassured her, I can't say; but her cries ceased, and the field was silent save for the sigh of wind in long summer grass and the distant drone of the sea.

The Devil's Darning Needle

Something was crawling out of the water, up the trunk of an alder tree. It was like a small prawn, greyish but uncurved.

It was the larva of a dragonfly, called Devil's Darning Needle in Devon.

After a year of underwater pursuit of other insects, and the fry of salmon, trout, and elvers, it was preparing to quit one element for another. All its life in backwaters and eddies had been a preparation for solar life of brittle and flashing splendour: to which life it now was crawling.

It stopped under a dried patch of fungus on the bark of the alder, and became fixed there. It did not move; and yet there was movement within the shell. It was pulling itself away from its old life. Legs, eyes, thorax, body, tail, were being urged away from themselves by an irritation of new power that caused it to strain and twist, until it broke away.

However, it had not gained freedom. It was still shut away from sunlight, which for the first time in its life was to be sought, not avoided. Its head, with the rapacious mandibles, could turn as though pivoted. Forcing it round in the mask which was becoming more brittle every moment it bit with its mandibles and strained to reach the sunlight.

When the mask was dry it split, and at once a different being began to tear a way out. It walked away, unsteadily, then clung to the fungus with its six legs, which were set with hooks to the knees. It was colourless, flaccid, unmoving.

An hour later it was holding four tremulous wings to the sun. In the first hour of its freedom the wings had sprouted and uncurled to crinkle and quaver as the sun poured its fierceness into their network of nervules which strengthened the membranes. And while it quivered there, drawing life and colour from the golden dragon of the sun, it felt the need for movement, and with a sudden rustle of wings was away on its first flight.

Its luminous eyes, with their many facets, quested a crinkling sheen like to itself: another dragonfly. It was a dark metallic green, drawn from the fiery breath of the sun, which made it swift and fierce with the very heat and light of life. Its globular eyes were inpouring with sunlight; they fixed upon other winged flight, its prehensile mask moved forward from its face, it pursued and snapped it, clipping off wings and legs and tearing its prey and swallowing it.

In flight it met another like itself, and the mating was fierce and selfish, like all its life.

Wings and mandibles of other male dragonflies clashed by it, and the female drew all that came. Her wings burnt to a darker green; until the fire passed from them, and she clung to the alder below the phantom of her old life.

Then she was rising and falling over the eddy, dipping her tail into the water at each fall and rising again to lay another egg. About a hundred times to the minute she dipped thus, minute after minute, until at last she faltered and flew erratically, hit a twig and fell into the water, exhausted.

With weak flutters she drifted down with the current and slid over the waterfall and was gone.

An Exmoor Holiday

From time to time Refereaders* write to me for information on all sorts of things, from the finding of lodgings for their summer holidays to demands for private articles on the life and habits of the late T E Lawrence.

I propose, therefore, to open periodically a bureau for information, in which I shall reply to those of my correspondents whose questions and, I trust, the answers to them, merit general interest.

Let us begin with a young gentleman calling himself Basil, from Streatham, SW16, whose letter, I suspect, is partly a decoy to find out where material for another page of his autograph book has its existence.

Basil says: 'I am in dire need of answers to the following questions, as I intend, within the next fortnight, to leave dreary London far behind and spend a week or so wandering on and around your Exmoor.'

But now to your questions: (a) Are snakes plentiful enough to be a real danger?; (b) Would leather leggings and boots assure immunity from harm?

To the first question (a) the answer is No; but vipers do exist, and are usually seen on sunny banks facing south, or on open patches amidst heather. They are more frightened of men, if possible, than men are frightened of them, and will always skedaddle from footfalls. Should they be surprised or interfered with, even accidentally, they will strike. The remedy is to cut the bite with a knife and apply permanganate of potash.

---

*Editor's note: The name by which The Sunday Referee liked to call its readers. In similar vein each issue was accompanied by a 'Special Referadio Supplement'.

Now for question (b): Leather leggings and boots in this sort of weather would surely be most uncomfortable, and what protection they would give from horseflies is outweighed (as serious writers say) by their appearance, especially if worn with shorts and a bowler hat.

Basil concludes: 'As this holiday has mainly a literary aim, I wish it to be as peaceful as possible; for this I should be most grateful.'

Well, Basil, as my holiday has a totally unliterary aim, and as I also wish to be as peaceful as possible, I shall be away from home for the next fortnight.

Now for another letter – from Gwen W., of Ashford. Gwen wants to know 'Do owls kill swallows?'

As I opened her letter two white Leghorn hens' feathers fell forth. These are enclosed as possible evidence against a white owl.

Gwen says: 'I am very sad today as a swallow built a nest in our church porch and used to sing when we sang the hymns. She was hatching her babies, and today I find that the nest is pulled down and the brave little mother all eaten, except her head and wings, and the eggs scattered about. It is probably the work of cats, but there are large white feathers about which look like hens' feathers, so it might be a white owl; but someone tells me that they are the large feathers of the swallow. What do you think?'

I should think it was the cats. Rats would eat the eggs and boys would take them, but in fairness it should be added that rats practically never go into churches, and that modern boys are not so destructive as they were.

Some Secrets of my Day's Work

The sun now is my only clock. I get up from the little loft-bedroom of the hut when the sun shines in my eyes through the open window, between seven and eight in the morning.

Dressing does not take long: off with pyjamas, a pail of water poured over head and shoulders, quick towelling, and on with a pair of shorts. I am ready for the day's work.

After typing a page or so just to break myself in to the job (imaginative creation is unnatural, and writing, either words or music, the most vicious of the arts for the body), I light the fire of sticks under the kettle and go and scythe a few more yards of docks and thistles.

After breakfast of toast and eggs and my own lettuces and radishes, I sit in the sun, now hot, wearing dark glasses and typing a word now and again. I have only the vaguest idea of what to say, and as the sun mounts higher a greater desire to loll on the log before the small green baize table and close my eyes.

There are moments when a flow of words starts; this is exciting, or at least satisfying momentarily. Then I have to resist the desire to wander off round the field, looking into this or that nest, or scything, lazy as a negro in Georgia, a few more thistles and docks.

So I sit, hotter and hotter, getting browner and browner, typing slower and slower, but always working.

It must be about eleven o'clock; so let's go into the hut and have a drink of home-made lemonade. Heavens, it's nearly half-past four; and less than a thousand words done.

Time for lunch. Food is a nuisance; a pity one can't be fed through the skin, by the sun's rays.

What's that? A bird fluttering at the window. Its mouth is

open; it gapes with fear or thirst. How long has it been inside, and the door open, too?

It is a whitethroat; exhausted. It flutters feebly from me, but perches quivering on my finger, and, shielded by the hand against hurting itself by dashing into glass, is carried to the open door, and flies off, scolding me.

Its mate joins it, and she waits in an ash sapling while the cock bird collects a beakful of brown flies, and feeds her while she shivers her wings at him. Charming scene!

Then while I am eating cheese and tomatoes within, and thinking of the bathe I shall be having soon, the open door reflects splashing noises.

A thrush is cooling itself in the water trough outside. He sometimes hops in to see me. I feed his (or her) young in a nest two yards away, fixed in a young spruce.

The bird looks on, eyeing the food from a foot or so away. It has almost overcome its fear of me; and before my book is done, or the weather breaks, I hope it will take food from my hand.

The Birds Vanish from their Sanctuary

When last I wrote at this small green baize table, out of doors, and almost naked to the heat of the sun, the field and the growing trees about me held many small birds.

They whistled, sipped, scolded, whurred, piped, clucked, and made many other sounds of alarm and anxiety; for scores of fledgelings were in their care.

This field, as you may recall, is on the top of a hill, and the trees are the only trees for some distance.

I do not cut the grass, except to scythe docks, thistles, ragworts – all 'noxious weeds within the meaning of the Act' which demands their cutting by all owners of land. (Very few observe this law, and probably there has never been a prosecution under it.)

I don't cut the weeds because the law demands it, but because I don't want the land to 'go back', as farmers say. The tall grasses left give shelter to much insect life; and as there is also drinking water in the field and cover among low trees, it is a bird sanctuary.

Insect food this year, owing to the fine weather, is abundant. One missel-thrush, nesting in a small pine five feet high, laid three sets of eggs all in the same nest. The last clutch, as a set is called, was forsaken. There were three eggs instead of the usual four. I imagine the bird became suddenly bored.

Other birds in the field used their nests for new broods also. I found a robin, two thrushes, a blackbird, a hedgesparrow, and a whitethroat doing this. Such a thing is most unusual; and all caused by the plentiful food. The birds were too lazy to make new nests, or, rather, the hens, stimulated by rich feeding, were ready to lay again as soon as the first broods were away.

I went away for a few days and returned yesterday. Today,

writing this in the heat and blaze of the sun, the only sounds in the field are of flies, grasshoppers, and motor-cars.

The birds are gone. Where? To the shade of valleys and ground less hard and hot.

Perhaps the rhythm of early summer insect life is dying down, being replaced by flies which are too fast to be caught. The air around me is scored with shooting vibrations of crisp wings, all of flies which lay their eggs on carrion – the blowflies, green Spanish flies, and those larger speckled flies whose buzz, if they are caught in the hollow of the hand, is almost painful.

As for the motor-cars, they are passing all day and half the night, up and down the hill to and from the north coast and Ilfracombe. Every hundred yards on the hot road surface of bitumen and granite chip there lies a flat wad of skin and feathers, remains of some of the younger birds which were reared on the edge of this little wilderness.

Gulf Stream Brings Strange Visitors to Devon

Strange jelly-fish are lying on the wet sands, left there by the receding tide. They are striped with brown on their feelers; and brown divides their bodies into segments.

I last saw jelly-fish like these on the sands of the Gulf of Mexico. Have they come to Woolacombe Bay, North Devon, with the Gulf Stream?

For something has happened to the currents in the bay. From Woolacombe Down you see the currents marked by smooth wandering tracks, as though great snails had glistered them. And when swimming along the edge of the sea, almost waveless but unclean, alas! with newspapers and other litter left by the happy careless crowds, you are suddenly stricken by chill water which surely comes from icebergs melting off Labrador.

Swim on a few strokes, and you are in water almost hot. This is at low tide, before the water has run over sands heated by the day's sun. This warm water is surely from an overflow of the Gulf Stream, which is a constant 60 degrees Fahrenheit. It is the Gulf Stream that brings back the trillions of elvers from their hatching place in far Sargasso to the rivers of Europe.

I have not known such a summer since the Great Drought of 1921, when no rain fell between April and August, when some of the pasture fields on the headland were dry to the rock, the grass like coconut matting.

A terrible time it was for sheep. I remember one running down the street of Croyde village, its eyes staring mad, its sun-dried coat flapping on its raw sides.

But all that is forgotten in the joy of swimming. The sea is as clear as Cornish water, since only the smallest trickle is coming down the rivers.

One is in the tropics, sun-charred. Only in solar freedom does the body release the mind, to become the silver-flicker and yellow sand-shadow of ripples.

It is the loveliest feeling to swim slowly into the hot sun, eyes closed, poised without body between sleeping and waking; or to glide along glassy water and see one's hands as though for the first time, fore-shortened and strangely pink in a mesh of green and gold, moving in and then exploring forward beyond sight, to return and weave their underwater patterns of independent life again.

Down there the tiger-barred jelly-fish expands and contracts, as though wondering at the strangeness of sand.

Does it know its fate? To be left high and dry by the next tide; to be slain by the sun, to dwindle to a mere dry shapelessness: to receive absolution, and return to its beginning.

Dawn over Exmoor

Soon after dawn, which I saw through the narrow window of the tallat or loft where I had been sleeping all the summer, partridges began to call in the next field.

At the same moment gulls, dark against the dusky distinctness of the eastern sky, flew slowly across. They had come from their roost in the cliffs of the headland two miles away, and were peering, owl-like, for any maimed or crippled rabbits squatting in the hayfield. The banks were almost hollow with rabbits' burrows.

The three gulls came at the same time or light every morning, and flew always the same way and at the same height above the ground. Other gulls were patrolling other fields.

A wild gabbling cry broke out of the darkness in the far corner of the meadow by the haystack: a gull had found something, and in its excitement had told the others.

The three dark streamlined shapes which had been returning tranquilly in formation over the bank dividing my field from

Farmer Bales' pasture became three winged reptiles hastening through air and screaming at one another in competition.

Now at midnight, coming to my hilltop hut, I had heard a rabbit crying down there; and a few minutes before that, driving up the lane in my car, I had seen a low shape crossing the lane swiftly in the beams of the headlights. It was so pale I thought it must be a ferret, and yet it was smaller, the shape of a stoat. Curious, for some time ago I had written a short story of a white stoat at this very place: and here was the white stoat.

The bank of earth and stone topped with beech and thorn and bramble dividing Jack Bales' field from mine was about a dozen yards away from the window through which I was staring with eyes that were still unclear from sleep. Presently, while I was waiting for clouds to move from the bright morning star, I heard the call of partridges nearer, so near indeed that through the open window the hen-like *gock gock gock* was distinctly loud.

After awhile a mottled movement as of dead leaves on the top of the bank among the beech saplings and the brambles made me stare and blink (not daring to move a knuckle to my bleary eyes), and then I saw, not one bird, but another and another and another – and, yes, quite a score of birds were crouching on the bank, in line, and they were being kept so by the ordered clucking of the hen bird, whose upright neck and head on the flank of the covert revealed her anxious authority.

The cockbird stood, also sentry-like, on the other flank. Both birds were speaking to their grown children, telling them to wait there until it was safe to cross into the next field.

For about a minute they waited there, until a cautious *gock gock gock* made them follow the parent bird through the long grasses and knapweed stalks to the ground below. One close behind the other, the young birds, looking like tortoises, moved down the steep slope of the bank, and then, on the ground, they spread out in line again and began feeding.

The Lesson of the Spider

We knew that the weeks of wind blowing from beyond the beech clump standing to the north of the field were over at last when one morning spiders reappeared and began spinning their webs.

Walking among the little fir trees around the hut, one felt their lines press and snap against face, knees, and arms. These were the spiders generally called garden spiders: they make a web like the wheel of a cart. They were brown in colour, and of many patterns, spotted, striped, and blotched, some pale yellow, others dark as the trunks of the fir trees. All of them were females.

You have seen them in your gardens, of course. They sit in the middle of their wheel-webs, holding with the serrated claws of their eight feet, head downwards, waiting for fly, or bee, or grasshoppers to flip into their webs, the mesh of which is hung with globules of gum. They have several eyes in the front of their heads, glinting in some lights like tiny lamps, and also at their back, near the pouches or spinnerets where the silk line is stored and withdrawn, when needed, by rapid movements of their rear legs. They have two hollow fangs, like the horns of a bull, very powerful, with which they grip and rend and poison their prey, while rasping at its body with sets of teeth and suction discs which soon consume it, leaving it empty and shapeless, and black as though charred.

In fine weather and at night the spider sits in the centre of her web, awaiting the tremor which tells her that an insect has fallen into the snare. At other times she retires to a lair under a leaf or twig, where she has made herself a silken shelter; and there she hangs, as though asleep, the claw of one leg holding the main twisted line by which she will descend rapidly to the centre of the web when, by vibration, she knows something is entangled there.

There were hundreds of such webs in the field after the cold north-west wind had blown August away. At sunset, walking from the eastern hedge, I saw a luminous tunnel in the grasses between me and the sun. The whole field was gleaming with gossamers, which had floated there on the gentle west wind. The male lovers were arriving for the annual ceremony of courtship and, they doubtless hoped, marriage.

In the morning I saw them. They were small, thin creatures, with long legs and timid movements. They clambered about the grasses, sending their lines and parachutes into the wind and floating off on them in the hope of finding what they sought in the sky. They were never seen at any other time of the year; how they fed, if, indeed, they feed at all, is a mystery to me.

Meanwhile the females sat in their webs. I watched one diminutive and starved lover approaching a mistress. He was anxious and alarmed at his boldness. He stalked gingerly down one of the main supports of the web, tapping all the while with a forefoot.

The enormous female sat complacently or watchfully in the centre of her web, apparently indifferent to his arrival.

Minute after minute the emaciated wooer stalked towards her, tapping and feeling his way, while making sure of his retreat by drawing after him a line on which he could launch himself into space at the first rebuff. I felt relief when I saw the wretched wooer had prepared a get-away, for I knew what he did not know – yet.

Gradually he approached the centre of the web, his foot beating *accelerando agitato*. She waited, quite still. He paused, exhausted; or perhaps his nerve had failed him. But love was stronger than death, and he went on.

Tap tap tap, are you ready, my love? he seemed to be jazzing.

At last he dared to approach her, but fear overcame passion, and he let go just in time, as her forelegs crooked out to embrace him and those bull-like horns opened wide for a satanic embrace. Down he swung, then up he scrambled again, the loose line tangled on his hind claws. Again with relief I observed that he had the good sense to tack a fresh life-line to the web before approaching her again.

So it went on for about half an hour, while he wooed her by the Morse code, as it were, sending telegram after telegram, possibly telling her he meant no harm to her whatsoever, but to trust him, he wouldn't let her down, he had come a long, long trail to see her, he loved her, he, &c., &c.

While she waited, her eyes glinting, giving nothing accepting everything, letting him do all the work and have all the anxiety and hope and exaltation and despair: and then, to my horror – and, if I may use an Americanism which seemed appropriate to the occasion – she *gave him the works*.

In what old-fashioned writers would call *a trice*, she had him gripped and twirling in a shroud of silk and glue, helplessly bound; while the horns plunged into his tangled body and those teeth rasped away the life of the poor little aerial dreamer.

As for the moral of this cynical but truthful account, I can think of none, unless it be: Wait till they are old enough – and then don't.

Autumn

Summer Passes

In the calm blue air a sparrowhawk wheeled over the field, cutting an arc through the lens of my glass with wings which shone at the turn like the yellow grasses in the sunlight.

It was so quiet on the hilltop that the cries of swallows dashing at the hawk seemed to come from just above the clump of beech trees; whereas even with the eight magnifications of a Zeiss lens, I could not distinguish the whitish patch on each breast. It was not the bird of prey that excited them, I guessed. They were playing through the empty corridors of the sky – empty for them now that they were awaiting the tribal sign for migration.

The swallows flew swiftly and excitedly above the sparrowhawk, which wheeled amidst a continuous twitter. Calmly the hawk soared, tracing a flat spiral across the sky. Sometimes one of the tiny winged specks seemed to hurl itself on it, and then to flick up again hurriedly to the agitated throng above.

I watched until the birds were out of sight behind the beech trees.

Grasshoppers were risping in the warm grasses; the drone of the flying-school aeroplane, carrying the last of summer's pupils, came from away over Exmoor.

I sat in the sunshine, trying not to think how in a few days the beech plantation, cut by Atlantic winds to the shape of a porcupine, the topmost boughs stripped and killed by the salt blasts, would be black and bare, its last brown leaves streaming away in the wind.

And the swallows, which were roosting in thousands every evening among the reeds of the duckponds down below in the grazing marsh, would be flying under the sun of Africa. It was the end of summer.

These few calm days before the gales of the equinox are very lovely. In the cold mirk of dawn the constellation of Orion bestrides the southern sky. Orion is a winter star-group; the Hunter has arisen. Was that hoar frost this morning in the grasses, or was it a heavy dew?

Awaking early, before partridges were calling, I got down from the tallat and, opening the door, walked into the last of the night. The waves on the sands of Croyde Bay three miles away were roaring in the dawn. The morning star was a bead of red gold beyond the mists of Exmoor.

At every step the long, rough grasses of the field, uncut for two years, scythed my feet. Rabbits rustled through the hedges. An owl was suddenly wide-winged and dark over my head, and I saw two feathers like horns above its eyes as it floated past like the spirit of silence.

The first of the autumn migrants had arrived from Scandinavia.

Light came full and wide, but Silence remained. Ruddy vapours over Dunkery Beacon quenched the morning star, and when the sun rose I saw the tracks of sheep over the field, distinct and green among the dew-white grasses, with the smaller tracks of rabbits.

Vainly I searched for mushrooms; the last one had been picked by the last summer visitor.

So I sit in the sun, writing this article, drowsily, having walked for several hours since the first light of this morning, lured by summer's final beauty.

Leaping the Weir

Last Sunday the children and I went down to Stag's Head weir, hoping to see salmon leaping. The water was not high enough, however, although rain had been falling heavily on Exmoor that morning.

We waited by the main falls for half an hour, seeing only two sea-trout, one of them about a pound in weight, the other about six ounces. The silver sea coat of these fish was tarnished, and so we knew they had been in the river for several weeks.

Before we set out to the weir my son John, aged five, informed me that fish were not running. He said he had seen the herons standing beside the river higher up the valley, beside smooth water. He said that if the fish had been below the falls the herons would have been there, too.

His fond father was delighted with the child's perception and reasoning, although this delight was lessened somewhat when John said that that was what his father had told him a year before.

No more fish appeared, and we thought we would go and look at the spillway or overflow of the leat which fed the water-wheel a hundred yards away through the wood.

A leat, by the way, is the stream or conduit which glides from the weir-pool, made by the damming of the river, and flows along a prepared bed to the fender which regulates the weight and volume of water falling on the buckets of the mill-wheel.

Taking off shoes and socks and rolling up trousers, I walked along the sill of the weir, carrying the protesting John. The water was only about three inches deep, but it made my feet ache. The flat stones of the sill were slippery, so it was necessary to walk with caution.

When protesting daughter Margaret had been carried over we

went along the path through the brambles and over a narrow plank beside the iron doors at the head of the leat, and along another path towards the saw-mills. Here everything was quiet.

We crossed the leat again by a narrow bridge made of two planks laid together, and so to the island where the sawdust is dumped among pines and rhododendrons. Then we came to the spillway or overflow of the leat and sat down and watched the thin, white water on the stone face of the spillway.

We had not been there a minute when a sea-trout as long as John's arm, but ever so much fatter, swam up from below and started to thresh violently up the spillway. More than two-thirds of its body showed above the ragged fleeces of the water. Halfway up it lay on its side exhausted before being washed down again into the rivulet below.

Then another smaller fish swam up and rested in a tiny eddy just below the spillway made by an old and rusty scythe blade wedged there. We sat still and watched this fish edging slowly up to the beginning of the slanting white fleece of water before giving a leap and threshing up in what looked like a series of leaps.

This little fish got to within three feet of the top, and then clung with its paired fins to the stem of a dock which was growing between the crevice of two stones. There it rested nearly a quarter of an hour, its tail curved round the base of the dock.

Just above it was a turbulent pool about as big as my foot, made by the dislodgment of one of the stones. With a sudden spring and violent flicker the fish was in this pool and lying there with its brown tail out of the water.

Bird Migrants of the Stratosphere

A friend from Australia came to see me yesterday, and while we were discussing the migration of birds, he told me of a belief that is held by many of the 'cockies', as farmers are called down under.

A few years ago, before theories and practices of modern aircraft and terms like stratosphere opened up a new world in the sky, this belief would have been as amusing as the older belief among countrymen that swallows in the autumn dived into the mud of ponds and rivers and remained there until the next spring.

This is what my friend told me: 'The cockies say that when certain birds, notably the black shag, which I believe is the name given to the cormorant, want to travel to some distant portion of the globe, they do not fly there but fly straight up beyond the range of the earth's gravitation and stay there until the earth has come round to the place they wish to visit. Then they swoop down to it. A curious idea, but one which is seriously thought to be true. I was speaking of birds to a cockie just before I left Australia in July last, and he it was who told me of this, and cited an experience of his which made me believe it to be a fact.

'He was lying on his back one fine day above a sizable lake, and staring up into the sky in which nothing was to be seen. No sign of birds or clouds or anything. Suddenly he became aware of an infinitesimal black speck far away up in the sky, only just discernible, so distant was it. As he watched, it grew in size until he could easily see it as a black speck in the sky.

'It grew and expanded until finally it turned into an endless flock of birds. Do you remember those starlings we watched years ago near Merton, flying into that ten-acre plantation of larch trees, which they had killed by the act of roosting there? And how hot it was from the mass of the perching birds, when we walked under the bare trunks of the trees after sunset? Well, the cockie estimated that there were scores of thousands of black shags descending from the sky, pouring out of the blue at a terrific pace. They dived down vertically, apparently simply dropping, and when about two hundred yards from the surface of the water they opened their wings and swooped on to the lake. The water was simply lousy with them, to use his own homely expression. It was a big lake, several square miles of water, and he could scarcely see any water at all for the shags.'

By the description of the dive and the suggested speed of flight the birds seemed to me to be loons, or black-throated divers. Cormorants or shags have a slow broad-winged flight, powerful, but not very fast; while the loon goes through the air as though streamlined in black glass. So I have seen them flying in Florida, and also over the lakes of Eastern Canada; looking as though they could fly backwards with equal speed, as their legs behind appear to be the shape and size of their sharp-beaked heads in front.

Be the bird shag, cormorant, or diver, the speculation is: Do they migrate as the cockie believed?

The air is very thin and cold even at 20,000ft., which is miles below the realm of supposed non-gravitational pull. Such birds could reach that height, but would not they suffer from cold? Or find breathing difficult? And why should they rise so high?

By the evolutionary processes observable within any bird's egg, we know birds were once reptiles: that they came from the sea originally, and not from the air. Therefore no ancestral memory or instinct would take them so high; and no later desire for food, since their food has always been on land or in water.

Why, then, should they fly high at all, I wondered. Well, at a mile high, when these birds would be invisible from the ground, there is often a wind when the air near the earth is calm.

I suggest that the cockie lying on his back (the sort of attitude I should choose whenever possible were I a farmer) would have seen those birds approaching had there been an adverse wind between four and five thousand feet.

The Doomed Elm Tree

The old polled elm tree in Braunton is doomed. Braunton is the largest village in England; and although it does not know it, Braunton is doomed too.

For years the tree stood at the junction of these roads, and much gossiping spittle was squirted around its base. Its lower bark was stuck with rusty nails, where in olden times notices were fixed. In autumn moonlight I have seen the trunk glistering with silvery tracks, for within its hollow many snails slept in winter.

Nowadays the spittle around its base is mixed with oil from motor-cars. First one new road was made, then another. Five ways now meet beside the Cross Tree.

The old elm tree is doomed. Not so much because the rubber wheel is everywhere replacing the iron-hooped wooden wheel, but because the local Council – which caused the ugliest, stupidest, most disgusting fence of corrugated iron sheets with saw-edge tops to be erected in front of apple orchards when one of the new roads was built, has decided to cut down its old tree.

The Council bickers, gives and takes offence; nearly all its members are self-seekers, ambitious men wishing to serve their own interests. When they come to questions of what is called 'public good', they are as ingenuous and bewildered, products of a repressive and stultifying education.

Why cannot a traffic-lights standard be put beside the tree, which stands well back from the streams of motor traffic? Ah, but where is there precedent for a traffic-lights standard erected beside an old elm tree?

Precedent, that's it, a master word. Precedent.

''Tes modern times, that's it midear; tidden like old times, 'tes all this yurr progress, 'tes modern, whether us likes it or not, these yurr motors have come vor bide, us must keep up with the times, mustn't us? So us votes that the old tree be cut down.'

Braunton wants to be a town. It does not care in the least that it is the oldest and the largest village in England. It wants to grow with the times. Indeed, it is almost a town already – a formless, modern, jerry-built nonentity, a suburb of London. Regard this great glaring public house, without atmosphere or personality, which replaced the snug little old Railway Inn.

It might have come from the Old Kent Road, built in 1896. What mind inspired those shining black factory-made panels beside the door, advertising somebody's beer? I shall never drink beer there. I'll drink water, although even the local water, a resident doctor tells me, is liable to rot the teeth.

As for the local sanitation, the largest village in England has the simplest sewage system and the filthiest. It's illegal, too, like Barnstaple's open sewer, 'contravening' the Public Health Acts. Just a straight pipe pouring into the pill or creek at the edge of The Great Field. There it is, where the gulls are screaming. How many salmon smolts and little sea-trout does this gut of human ineptitude poison every year?

You may ask, after this outburst, Is the Cross Tree a danger to modern traffic? If it be, then surely it is wise to cut it down, since human life is, by general agreement, more valuable than arboreal life?

The answer is, No, it is not a danger. It is well back from the road. And I repeat, traffic signals can be put in various other places. It is simply that the communal or representative mind dealing with the affairs of the village is the sort of mind that, seeing a white wren or thrush or other rarity, has this immediate reaction, Shoot it, and have it stuffed.

So the tree is doomed.

Just a Bridge

There is a bridge over one of the smaller rivers of Dartmoor which is only a few feet wide; but looking over the parapet, one is surprised to see the river running a long way down in the earth. Thin moss-covered trees cross the black cleft in the rock.

The river, flowing through thousands of centuries, has slowly ground its pot-holes deeper and deeper. The rock might have been of rustless iron; but the power of falling water is everlasting.

By paying sixpence to an old man with a squeaky voice and brackeny appearance who is usually to be found standing by the gate, you can walk down the path into the gorge itself. The slight momentary feeling of resentment for having to pay sixpence to walk beside a river departs when one has gone a few yards into the gorge, and sees that the charge is justified, if not indeed necessary, for the upkeep of the iron rails, the stout wooden bridges, and for the maintenance of the paths which often fall away in the winter months.

In summer the best part of a day should be spent down the gorge, strolling, listening, idling, and watching. In summer the river is low and clear, and if you keep still, you will see the trout lying just under the surface of the water watching for the flies which drop from the trees and bushes.

Most of the people who come down the gorge arrive by motor-coach and walk all the way down and then all the way back with few rests. If you do it this way you will certainly get the exercise you probably need; but the best way of all is to arrive on foot, free of the world, without need for constant wrist-watch glancings.

In places you will see where the river has cut through the rock in a series of water formations like cauldrons one below the other. The water is always cold, even in the hottest summer. You pass through a tunnel, blasted through rock, and below the tunnel the gorge gradually widens. The sides of the valley above are less steep, and wooded deep. Scrub oaks grow up to the sky, and ravens flying just over the tops of the highest trees look no bigger than sparrows, so deep is the valley.

If you follow the river down, you will have a feeling like that of Bevis and Mark, while exploring the New Sea in that grand book by Richard Jefferies, which has recently been reprinted with illustrations by Mr E H Shepard – and to me these illustrations seem precisely right.*

I came here last week, and lay beside the river on a dry bank of gravel, and dozed, feeling myself an echo of water-music and rippled sunshine. Suddenly there was a shriller chittering, and as I sat up I had a glimpse of a small black and white bird diving into the water. It was an effect most curious – that of the disappearance of the bird with the sudden cessation of its crying. Almost instantaneously a larger brown bird, with a grey-black barred breast, swished by within a foot of the water; and seeing me, it swerved and slipped through the ash-poles.

A few minutes later I was watching the dipper's blurred pied image moving through the still water before me. The bird appeared to be pulling itself along the river bed, clasping small stones with its feet. It walked out of the water and I sat as still as possible, while it shook itself, gazed at the sky with first one eye and then the other, and broke into a song of joy, as clear and bright and sharp as the water-sparkles on the shallows beyond.

Editor's note: This edition of *Bevis: The Story of a Boy* was published by Jonathan Cape in 1932, price 7s. 6d.

In Praise of Brighton

For the writer, a creature who usually lives more within himself than the majority of his fellow men, too much solitude is as injurious to his ideas as too much social congestion.

By solitude I do not mean full employment of time when alone; but idle rumination and inactivity, for that is what solitude usually means to the writer. A year or two ago, feeling that the solitude of my valley life was becoming stagnancy, and stagnancy being death, I departed for New York, the noisiest place I could think of, in order to find stimulation for fresh work.

That was the swing of the pendulum; and I learned from the six months living alone in an apartment, unfurnished except for bed, chair, and table, that life in a great city could be more lonely than a moorland valley.

I still live in the moorland valley, but the loneliness has gone, because I have learned to live more like a normal or natural man. My days are planned.

Wild animals (which live a marvellously happy life, full of fun and excitement and interest, usually ending with enviable abruptness) are creatures of the most regular habit. Their days, or nights, begin at the same time, judging by the sun, which is their creator. They do the same useful things usually in the same places and along the same tracks. Their lives are organised.

Many writers sneered at the late Arnold Bennett for organising himself, for regarding himself as a fiction-factory; but he was, in his regular and sensible habits, less unnatural than most of those writers who haunt the Café Royal night after night, where they sit hoping to be recognised and hating it when someone stares at them, waiting there hour after hour, either trying to convert their companions into their own artistic images, or, what is more usual, looking round most of the time in the hope of seeing something interesting – which never happens.

It is an admirable place to take one's grandmother, who must not be stimulated too much.

When the valley is too silent, Brighton is the place for me.

When frosts have 'put down' all the fish in the river, when hour after hour the only movement is of water, and coloured leaves of the forest turning and drifting, oak and elm and alder and sycamore, in eddy and waterfall and pool, then I reach for helmet and goggles and leather coat, and in my open car feel the south coast of England dissolving under me and the rush of sea wind on my face.

How comfortable and sweet a place is Brighton, after the metallic rigors and stridors of New York! No one bumps into you, lurching with fatigue and the over-muchness of that cruel and brilliantly sordid city of the New World.

New York has its beautiful sights, such as the Radio City Building flood-lit at night; a work of art, indeed. But the softly flood-lit Brighton Dome seen through trees hung with festoons and chains of coloured bulbs, for the first time the other night, was equally beautiful.

Those grand buildings in New York owe their wonder to their towering height above streets of noise and congestion and monoxidic inhumanity; they are like snow-peaks, remote from life; they are beautiful but inhuman.

The lights of Brighton give a human welcome – they are soft and leisurely; the quaint and almost primitive traffic signals of wood, worked by policemen in little control tubs, have the friendliness of wooden toys.

Let us hope that Brighton will not scrap them for New York signals; and further, that Mr Hore-Belisha will never be the guest of Sir Harry Preston. This is inevitable, of course; so let me hasten to suggest that his yellow globes would look extremely nice on the ends of the groynes. They might even attract an occasional flounder towards those melancholy anglers to whom nothing ever

In Praise of Brighton

happens, except that their boot-stitchings are regularly rotted by the salt water.

A poor joke, you say? I don't care; I enjoy myself in Brighton.

You should have been with me last evening, as the tide was roaring high on the shingle beach towards midnight.

Pleasantly stimulated (much to my surprise) by the terrific villain of the film 'Chu Chin Chow', and pleased by the way my new book was writing itself, I walked with a friend along the front, coat buttoned up against the gale and hands thrust into pockets.

On the groynes and jetties the waves were breaking, throwing up irregular fans of water and spray fifty feet into the air.

We crept down one jetty, ready to run back should a monster ninth-wave suddenly rear itself over the Western wall. The feeling of apprehension was fine; our lips were salt with spume; we forgot ourselves in the white thunder of the sea and the appalling roar of shingle torn by each backwash.

Waves nearing the shore sometimes met the returning impulse of backwash; then they threw up white antlers and paws and rocked momentarily in collision before hurling themselves to the common assault of the shore.

This would not have been fun on the 'natural' Atlantic coast at night. The scene would have been too inhuman, too chaotic, without meaning.

But here in Brighton, in the lights of promenade and building, it was stimulating and enjoyable.

The Ducks

Soon after the windmill and granaries were burnt down in 1914, two wild ducks appeared on an old pond in Kent. They soon became tame, and would waddle swiftly to the miller's back door for the grain he threw to them. They were known to visit other back doors in the neighbourhood for food.

In the spring of 1915 each duck made her nest at the edge of the mill pond. Regularly at sunrise and sundown they would fly the same way over the fields, quacking and searching for a drake. All that spring and summer they sat on eggs which could not hatch, since parthenogenital miracles apparently do not occur among the lower mammals and birds.

The next spring, 1916, the same search at sunrise and sunset; so the miller, who didn't like to see good ducks wasted, bought a tame drake and turned him loose on the pond. The two ducks followed the drake so assiduously, never letting him alone, but quacking at him and pecking the curled feathers of his tail, that the drake flew away from the pond, and never came back.

During the years between 1917 and 1933, the ducks lived on the pond, spending about four months of each year brooding on eggs which eventually were forsaken, to be eaten by hedgehogs. The edges of the pond were littered with derelict nests and ancient shells.

In the winter of 1933–34 the old millhouse received two new tenants, young ladies with warm hearts and feelings, who gave the ducks the names of Jemima and Dolly.

In the spring of 1934, moved to pity by the vain search of the ducks for a drake, the two young ladies hastened to the market town and bought a young drake. They clipped his wings, lest he, too, try and avoid his responsibilities; and then he was released into the pond.

Round and round the pond he went, pursued by the excited and almost hysterical ducks. With straining neck he whimpered his alarm at the persecution. In the morning he was gone. A week later he was found on another pond a quarter of a mile away, whither he had walked, to join other waterfowl there.

Left together again, Jemima and Dolly fed and roosted together as before. But in February they were observed several times to be facing one another in the water, bobbing and bowing, and dipping their heads in the water faster and faster in unison. The ladies in the house went off to the market soon afterwards, returning with a clutch or set of mixed ducks' eggs. These eggs were put under Dolly, who was broody.

One morning in April they saw Dolly on the pond, followed by seven ducklings of varying colours. The broodless Jemima tried to nip them, but Dolly chased her so relentlessly that she flew away and stayed away four days. She was seen during that time on a lonely pond about five miles away, all alone.

On the fifth day she returned, and was accepted at once by Dolly. During their expeditions across the pond, Dolly always led and Jemima always followed behind the string of ducklings.

Two of the ducklings were missing one morning, probably taken by an immense piebald cat, which every year kills the moorhen chicks which are hatched on the pond.

At nightfall Dolly led her family to the pond's edge and scrambled into an old cider keg lying on its side there. Jemima helped preen the ducklings, cleaning their featherlets for the night.

The tiniest duckling, who had a favourite rotten board in the pond, was always last; he made several attempts each night to roost alone on his rotten plank. At last all would be inside the keg, and then the family would settle down to sleep.

And there we will leave them, undisturbed.

The Sussex Downs

It was a good thought as we strode on the high ground that in less than a month the days would be growing longer, that the dank half of winter would soon be passed into a time of frost and wind and snow.

It is the dying of summer that makes the prospect of winter fearful, and here we were on the Downs enjoying ourselves as though it were summer again.

It is no good taking one's moods from Nature, waiting, as it were, for inspiration from outside oneself.

See, that blue flower gives the only living colour except that of the grass we have seen today. It is a field scabious, and is usually to be seen in mass when the June corn is reaching its topmost growth, waving in the wind with poppies and moon daisies. But here on the sward cropped close by centuries of sheep, the stalk of the blue flower is less than a quarter of an inch long.

Far away white smoke strays in the air, arising from a grey patch on the side of the hill. It is the vapour from a cement works – which are gradually taking the Downs to other parts of England.

In the vast misty hollow between the hills in front of us there travels a powerful sonority of sound which bores into the quietness of the winter day, and very soon we discern a speck that approaches at a great rate and reveals itself as one of the American monoplanes entered for the Melbourne race.

Silence again as we walk on mile after mile, and come to a furze brake where a thrush is singing as though it were April. We pass a dew-pond, and over the brow of the hill hear the sounds of many sheep bells. A young man with a large brown moustache, in whose eyes and voice is the harmony of life, tells us that the sheep are belled against loss in the sea fogs that drift over the Downs.

The Sussex Downs

We go down the side of the hill and near the bottom, where the ploughland begins, we see, under some elderberry trees, masses of white chalk which appear to have been tipped irregularly from various carts. Flints weighing several pounds have been rolled down the hillside a score of yards. Evidently there have been tunnellings into the hillside; but what animal or animals have made these tunnellings by removing quite fifty tons of material?

Many of the holes are disused; moss grows in them; across others old spiders' webs are spun. Kneeling down by one of the main tunnels, in use to judge by the chalk pressed by the passage of many feet, one sees a grey hair about two inches long, which, when rolled between the fingers, is found to be flat. The stubble of the cornfield below is a foot high and pressed down in many places, as though animals have been rolling there, making it necessary to cut the wheat with scythes. Is it a fox's hair? asks someone. The hair of a wild dog? suggests another.

Surely you recognise this hair? You held its equivalent in your hand this morning, judging by the smoothness of your cheeks. That is, unless you use paint-brushes to lather your chins with.

Come along, it is teatime, and the young author of that Sussex film, 'The Song of the Plough', is waiting with his seven children and beautiful wife, with a large plate of muffins beside his open hearth.

Editor's note: The 'young author' was Reginald Pound, who in the 1930s was the features editor of the *Daily Mail*. A journalist and biographer, and a fellow-member with Henry Williamson of the Savage Club, he was elected a Fellow of the Royal Society of Literature in 1953, and died aged 96 in 1991. 'The Song of the Plough', a drama in which a farmer is saved from ruin by winning the sheepdog trials, was made by Sound City in 1933, and re-released by MGM in 1939.

Are Animals Trained by Fear?

Recently a chairman of a bench of magistrates, presiding over a Court of Summary Jurisdiction, remarked to a farmer who was being fined for cruelty to a horse, 'You deserve to be jolly well sent to prison, and you will be if you appear here again for such an offence.'

The magistrate was an eager rider to hounds, and as such had a keen regard for the welfare of horses.

The alleged cruelty of the farmer consisted in leaving his pony, which had some affliction in the feet, to graze in a marshy grazing field. The farmer declared that he thought the soft, cool ground would be good for the horse's feet; he could do no more.

Most English people feel strongly about the welfare and happiness of animals, especially tame animals; and most English people do not consider that their actions may be cruel. If any actions of theirs are criticised or judged by others, they either dismiss criticism or judgment as unknowledgeable, or they suffer a feeling of having been misunderstood and misjudged.

These reflections arise from reading a little book recently written by Miss Helen Trevelyan called *Heaven's Rage* (The C W Daniel Co.: 1s.), with a foreword by Mr Frank Swinnerton, one of the most balanced and perceptive of contemporary writers.

Heaven's Rage is a perfervid attempt to bring to the notice of the public the cruelty alleged to be practised in the training of 'performing' animals for stage, cinema, and circus. Miss Trevelyan alleges that the basis of all such training is fear; in most cases physical torture, and always mental pain. The principle is that animals are enslaved and reduced to weariness and are forced to behave in an unnatural manner.

The roar of the lion in one case was, she asserts, produced by 'a device in the shape of a metal plate placed in the cage under the lion to which were attached electric wires.'

If you have ever laughed at a monkey band you may be interested in Miss Trevelyan's statement of the way it is engineered.

'Monkeys,' she says, 'are tied to their seats and the instruments are pulled and jerked from off stage by wires fastened to their bodies . . . the leader of the orchestra usually sitting on a revolving stool to which he is firmly secured . . . poked from off stage by means of long poles . . . he flies into ecstasies of rage. To an audience such anger is highly ludicrous.'

Says Mr Swinnerton: 'How can we be made to understand?' And he answers himself: 'I do not know. Like the keen huntsman who is offended by the suggestion that he is blameworthy, the animal-trainer indignantly denies that he is cruel. He does not mean to be cruel. He thinks he is not cruel. That is a kind of invincible ignorance; for he is a man without imagination. The only thing to be done, therefore, is to ask the public if it realises how the performances it enjoys are produced.'

Mr Swinnerton then says what many of the more intelligent of the rising generations have been thinking and declaring: 'Whatever is unnatural is wrong. The performances of animals on the stage are unnatural. If we all refused any longer to witness them they would cease.'

Perhaps Mr Swinnerton will not object to a paraphrase of his words: The performances are becoming uninteresting to more and more people because more and more people in the world do not have the pre-1914 mind which, in spite of the fearful pronouncements of the pre-War minded still in power, will before long vanish, with the natural, one might indeed say the benevolent, processes of age and dissolution.

After the Rain

This December has been one of the most unusual Decembers in the West Country within living memory. The nights have been like the nights of April and May.

And the rains! They began on the second day of the month, and have continued ever since, except during two bright mornings.

On the third day the river rose and swilled, a turgid brown, into the edge of the meadows, and on that night I saw in the headlights of the car otters on the roads, crossing to hillside rabbit burrows at three different places.

Next day a jetsam of twigs, leaves, and an occasional empty corked medicine bottle lay on the grass of the Deer Park a foot above the level of the grey-green water running fast and heavy down the valley.

The water kept its level, showing that the rains which had fallen on Exmoor had filled all the springs. Two days later the old edging of twigs and leaves, scratched over by pheasants seeking seeds, was being rocked by another and greater spate many yards over the banks of the river.

Over Exmoor the sky was dull grey. Tree trunks rode down the flood, tipping up over the weir and scaring the salmon lying in the eddies below.

When the water 'fined down' the river was still in high spate. In one place below the weir the water was a purple-brown with a mass of fish resting there, awaiting in the comparative calm of the backwash their turns to bore up against the white thunder in the centre.

One after another, sometimes two or three together, they leapt up and fell aslant and quivered, so it seemed, into the rushing glide of the solid water. Many were caught at the leap, flung over backwards, and swept away. These were the newcomers, testing the weight and direction of the various streams or jets of water.

Those fish which had determined the weight and flow of the easiest torrent leapt into it, and, as they gripped the water, began to swim up, just discernible as vague shapes moving up ever so slowly.

The water was too strong, and after a period varying between five and ten seconds they were exhausted; they turned on their sides and were hurled among the broken wave-masses below.

During a sunlit moment I saw a silver flash in the torrent, and a clean-run salmon leapt six feet out of the white upsurge, and fell with a splash into the swift glide of water.

It went up slowly and steadily, and I thought as the seconds passed, seventeen, eighteen, nineteen, it would never reach the sill or crest of the weir.

Now it seemed to be motionless, its back fin cutting the water with lines of spray and glistening water-drops. Then it was gone.

A minute later it leapt in the pool above, a lovely blue and white curve, an impulse of joy in life which was passed to me, and now, I hope, to you.

Winter

The Dweller on the Hilltop

Down there in the village, revealed in the darkness by a solitary light in one of the new Council cottages, they say that only a 'mazed' man would want to live on the top of a hill.

They say that the winds must blow everything away, and the usual remark is that it must be very cold up there.

This morning the sun was shining in clear air over the hill when the villages below were drowned under white mist filling all the valleys. And what exhilaration there is tonight for the dweller on a hilltop!

I can see the lights of Appledore and Bideford and the shore lights of Instow ten miles away and below. The lighthouse of Hartland Point flicks and swishes across Bideford Bay to the west, and the lights of Lundy flash like large stars. I can hear the sound of tides on this Atlantic coast as though night itself were roaring at the earth.

Walking down the hill to the village, a feeling arises in the breast that the earth indeed was created for man, that all the elements are his servants. One does not get this feeling when living at the bottom of a valley.

Halfway down the hill the flashes of Hartland lighthouse became dull; I was now beginning to enter the mist.

The young moon which had been clear-cut and purple-bright from the hilltop now looked like the corroded yellow horn of a black-bodied bull in the black clouds over Hartland.

The image was so startling that I stopped and leaned over a gate, watching the horn shrinking and the bull losing form and spreading darky down until the flashes of the lighthouse were put out, and the whooping bellow of its siren arose above the roar of the sea.

The Notebook of a Nature-lover

The lane was streaming with water, for all the hill springs had broken with the rains of the past fortnight. It was pleasant to walk on the gleaming roadway with the soft trickle and plash of water running everywhere.

And so I came to the village, a dark and starless place under dripping elms, and to the inn, where the eyes were hurt by the hard, bright light from a modern lamp, and the wall of heat momentarily seemed to stop the breathing.

'Like to be where you've just come from,' said the landlord.

Fisherman's Paradise

Although the main road to London – one hundred and eighty miles eastwards – runs through South Dulton, it is said that nothing ever happens in the place.

Four years ago an ox was roasted in the market place, in summer, during a fair arranged by the Town Council in the hope of attracting visitors; but nobody came to see it except the inhabitants, six hundred of whom stared apathetically at what to any stranger would have appeared a ghastly sight; and having stared, the six hundred sat down at one length or series of tables and ate slices of the ox with potatoes at eighteen pence the plateful.

Lest the above be interpreted as a criticism of the town's old-fashioned dullness, let it be stated immediately that South Dulton in one respect is 'in the van of modernity and progress'; it possesses that which exists elsewhere only in the dreams of Utopians; it had acquired the land adjoining half a mile of the river, and therefore the right to fish for salmon and trout, which it had generously given to everybody.

Free fishing for all comers: God made the fishes for Man; and here men had their rights.

The river is below the town. At the bottom of the hill the London road is carried by a bridge with a grey stone parapet. The bridge marks the upper limit of the free fishing. Immediately below the bridge is a high weir with a stone apron sloping too steeply for the ascent of any fish except in an extraordinary flood. Salmon and trout running up to spawn remain below the weir – in the water of the free fishing. And just below the weir stands the inadequate town sewage plant.

Motorists returning from Ilfracombe to London at night

usually slow up at the bridge, for the road bends beyond it. Occasionally one stops, attracted and puzzled by the strange flashing and dancing of lights in the valley below. Scrutiny reveals that the lights are moving, apparently in the river itself.

Perhaps there is a shout, a violent splashing and beating of the surface; there may be a dull explosion, and the noise of surging water. The sounds of quarrelling and the snarling of dogs are not unknown.

Here no keeper, hired by tyrannical landlord, can prevent men from taking their rights; no water-bailiff, hated agent of the Board of Conservators, dare show his face on the bank.

Dazed by the little searchlights, the 'red' salmon which has run up to spawn – its skin dark brown, its flesh infirm – lies close to the bottom of the pool while the gaff or wire-noose on the long ash-pole is moved nearer the tail, nearer and nearer, the gaff just below the ventral fin, the noose over the dark square tail – then jerk! Out he comes!

Keep an eye on him, for rogues abound; there are always folk ready to steal the work of honest men.

During days of summer, when the river is dead low and bright, small boys can be observed stalking the few tiny trout, mere fingerlings, that have come up from below.

Bare-legged and intent, each with a stick to which is attached a fine brass-wire noose, the boys creep after the darting fish until they are fatigued and cowed; the noose is worked over the tail, jerk! put it in the pocket and go after that other one. Only four inches long, and ungrown?

'Yes, but if I don't have'n someone else will, so I'll have'n first!'

'That's right, my boy. You look after yourself; no one else will.'

The Bravest of Birds

Recently I was playing darts in an inn called the Golden Grove at Chertsey, in Surrey. My host for the week-end told me something about the ancientness and literary association of the place – Dickens, Bleak House, &c. – but I was not listening.

I was thinking of what had been said a few moments before about a 'tommytit' that once had nested in the small oak letter-box fixed inside the door.

Had the bird brought off its brood, I inquired? Oh, yes, they said, casually. But surely the box wasn't used for letters during that time? Oh, yes, they said, casually, and went on watching the game of darts, and my friend went on telling me about Dickens, Bleak House, &c.

Now consider what they meant to the bird. The letter-box had an ordinary-sized slit for letters outside, and a hinged doorlet for their removal from the inside.

At least twice a day the small perky bird, with its blue and yellow-streaked head, would have envelopes, six or seven times its size, darkening the slit before falling aslant its head or nest.

Stop. Twice a day? Why should the innkeeper have such a regular mail? Be factual.

Well, sometimes letters would fall on the bird snuggling into her nest of moss, feather, fibre, hair, and wool containing anything up to twenty small white eggs spotted delicately with reddish-brown; a double thump would precede the avalanche and sooner or later the door would open and a hand fill the space above her head and cause her heart to beat violently in her breast.

For the first few days she would, when the letters dropped upon her, swell up and expel the breath from her lungs with a furious hiss, at the same time striking with her wings.

Two seconds later she would puff and hiss again, but not so violently. She might hiss a dozen times before being exhausted. But she would not shift off those eggs.

Tommytits otherwise blue tits or titmice (we call them 'ackymals' in Devon) are the bravest of birds – and one weighs less than an ounce.

I wondered to myself if such a thing would be possible in any country except England. In some countries the nest would have been flung out; in others, perhaps, the postman would not have knocked twice: he might have slipped the letters under the door.

But where save in England would the nest be left for purely benevolent reasons and the usage of the box continued exactly as though the nest were not there?

The Silent Sentinel at the Gate

As I passed down the lane, the attitude of the sheep seemed unusual; a sick beast, I thought. It was standing on a slight mound, made of a rubble of broken bricks and stones, amidst the mud of the farmyard.

It stood quite still, an odd-looking sheep, with a body almost rectangular in shape, and covered with thick wool. Every afternoon, as I walked down the road for my daily exercise, the sheep was standing on the mound by the five-barred gate.

The use of the word farmyard to describe the surroundings would be complimentary to the farmer, for really it was a small-holding, a very small-holding in fact. The 'farmhouse', a few feet back from the road, was made of corrugated iron sheeting on a frame of wood; a bare rectangular place, very small, built originally during the War for the gunners of an anti-aircraft battery. Zeppelins and Gothas used to fly over these fields, on their way to raiding London.

As for the farm, it consisted of one small field, and the outbuildings were a shed of decaying boards, patched with rusty iron strips of drums once containing bitumen for the repair of roads.

The winter sunlight reflected weakly in the hoof-holes of the one cow, one sheep, and one sow with litter, which made up the livestock of the farm. All around the doorway of the solitary outbuilding the watery mud was trodden, a depressing sight.

And alone on its mound the old sheep stood, its body shaped like a box, its head large and woolly, its eyes fixed on the closed door of the tin home of its owner.

One afternoon as I went by, eleven very small, very pink piglets were frisking round the sheep, which stood in exactly the same place, in the same attitude. The piglets obviously regarded the sheep as an old and valued friend, in whom they had perfect trust; for while two of them were rubbing themselves dreamily against its hind legs, a third was stretching up and licking its mouth, while a fourth dozed under its shelter, and the remainder were standing near it, during a pause in a game of hide-and-seek.

While I watched these merry little creatures, all so unconscious of the brutal and carnivorous world into which they had been born, the sow hidden in the shed gave a series of grunts. Immediately the piglets were (to use an expression which was the last thing in modernity soon after the discovery of the electric cell) galvanised into activity. The leg-rubbers abandoned their posts, the dozing one lifted up a pink snout and flicked a pink tail, the kissing piglet made several hops into the air, and all together they cantered down the slope, over the mud, and disappeared one after another in a hole under the unhinged and propped-shut door.

I heard grunts and squeals and the sounds as of wrestling coming from the shed; but the old sheep took not the slightest notice.

Was it mad, I wondered, walking down the lane the next day. Animals do go mad; I have seen sheep made crazy by parasites in summer. Perhaps its feet were painful – for sheep suffer from a disease called foot-rot – and it stood there day after day because it was the only dry place on the farm.

A few paces further along the road could be seen white sheets of water in the valley below, where the pasture lands were flooded to the distant Romney Marsh. All the ditches moved with water, even on this higher ground where always a keen wind was blowing.

Yes; perhaps the sheep suffered from foot-rot. One day, perhaps, some well-fed person of sensibility would pass this way, and see it, and inform someone in authority, when the farmer would, perhaps, be summoned for cruelty and fined, and an order made for the death of the sheep.

Then the little pigs would miss their grave and immobile friend, whose legs were rubbing-posts, whose body was a canopy, whose lips were tasty with the strange and thrilling juices of grass and mangel-wurzel.

I came to look for the rectangular woolly statue on its hillock during my afternoon walks. Always the glassy eyes, pale and suspicious and stupid, were fixed on the door of the farmhouse, with its garden scattered with tins and paper, unsifted cinders of coal, trodden and scratched over by chickens.

Did I say there were chickens on this farm? Nearly a score of them, lean-looking and scrubby, waited about on the thin grass and trodden mud, too dejected to scratch for what was not there. They were sad objects, devitalised and stupid by aimless living within man's protection during so many centuries. They, too, had lost the way of life: they were vicious, like all tamed creatures who live or exist without constant stimulation of the primitive feelings of fear and work and exploration.

And yet, like other civilised things, they had their moments of happiness. On my last afternoon, as I hurried along, trying to keep warm against the cold wind, I saw them huddled together around the old sheep on the mound. Four of them were perched on its back, and as I looked a fifth climbed up.

It was too much for the sheep. Its legs gave way and it lay down. Whereupon a sixth clambered on to its head.

A small pink snout peered under the rotten door of the outbuilding, and then trotted out. Immediately three of its pink brethren were beside it. As though they had received an order, they suddenly galloped across the mud, skittered to the mound, appeared perplexed by what they saw, and galloped back to obscurity within their rusty house.

On my way back, at twilight, the chickens were still there. Two lights moved across the dull sky, with the drone of an aeroplane. I hurried to my tea, wondering if I knew why farming in England did not always pay.

Stark Tragedy in Bird Land

My little boy came home from school in the twilight carrying something carefully in his hands. 'Look!' he cried, and held out a yellow bundle of feathers from which depended white legs with clenched claws and lolling head. Its eyes were glazed and shrunken. It was dead, a barn, or white, owl.

'Did anyone shoot it?'

'I don't know. I found it in the deer park, lying on the grass.' Anxiously the little boy held out his important find.

Taking it in the hand for examination, the first thing one noticed was its extreme lightness. Although the barn owl in flight looks twice – in some lights, thrice – the size of a pigeon, its body is no larger than a pigeon's.

Now, how had this owl died? It had not been shot, its wings were not broken, its breast was white as snow. But how light its weight – just a feathered skeleton. The boy said he thought one of its feet had been hurt.

One leg appeared to be broken in the thigh. The foot of the other was maimed; a toe was missing. The wound was half healed. The bird had died of starvation, after struggling in and escaping from a rabbit-gin.

During the winter more than a million gins must be 'tilled' every day in Devon. At twilight, as it lollops out to feed, a rabbit steps on a metal plate hidden in earth outside its hole. The pressure releases a catch, steel jaws snap together, lacerating if not breaking its legs, which are held by sinews. Twelve hours later the rabbit may be released and knocked on the head. Most of the North Devon rabbits supply the Birmingham markets.

My little boy and I talked of what had happened to the owl since it had escaped from the gin. At first, wild fright and freedom;

crooked and tottery perching on an oak branch, the owl falling off; then a rest spread-winged in the grass below.

Pain, bewilderment, glancing about in the grass for an unknown enemy.

Hunger, and after a painful take-off, in the air again. A mouse moving below; descent and grip upon the shadow; the mouse escaping. The owl falling over and flapping upright on useless feet.

A very hungry owl would seek its hollow oak, there to doze throughout daylight, hearing the movements of woodlice, shrews, even worms in the leaf-mould below. At sunset it would climb out laboriously and fly along its regular evening way.

It would catch no mice. There would be no beetles or moths in the grass of winter. . . .

Perhaps that thin, skirling cry we heard coming from the direction of Farmer Slee's haystack a night or two ago, when the constellations were so big and bright, was the death cry of the bird.

We saw an owl flying strangely, didn't we? Wan and irresolute in the wind it passed. We saw it from your bedroom window, do you remember?

Perhaps the owl did not see the stars, for death is a darkening of the sight, the world fading away.

On it flew, tumbling blindly and crying, to fall in the grass and sleep away from cold and the pain, until you found it and brought it home.

The Salmon-leap

Usually, migrating fish will not 'run' when the water of a river is rising. They show excitement, however, by leaping out and rolling along the surface above their resting places.

The river I have been watching for several years has been exceptionally low lately, and last November and December very few salmon were on the spawning redds. There was not enough water for them to ascend Stag's Head Weir.

Then all one night we heard rain pattering from the thatch.

How strange the river looked from the bridge, with the familiar stones of its gravel bed hidden, and hundreds of black-brown beech-leaves passing under the arches every second. The water looked good and deep, although not so high as one would have wished, but those clean-run fish in the estuary would now have a chance to run.

Those which had not already died of exhaustion after being a year in fresh water without feeding, and having exhausted themselves further by spawning, would face the currents and drift down, falling tail-first and fearfully over the weirs and rocks which might tear anew their sick and broken bodies.

As soon as the spate began to 'fine down' – that is, the washings from the road and field drain having run away, and river's brown turbidity changing to a fawn semi-opaqueness which in half a day would become grey-green 'running' water – I went to the Stag's Head Weir.

A heron flew up as I approached along the path under the hillside trees of the left bank. By that I knew fish were showing below the falls.

I watched, standing still, lest movement scare them as they waited in the eddies, avoiding the direct force of the white-bubbled streams. I could see a reddish-purple hue in the wavelet-rocked water between two streams. Six or seven, or perhaps more, salmon were waiting there. They were kelts.

As I stared, a fish of about fifteen pounds appeared on his side, as though sliding or toboganning *up* moving snow. I saw his deep tapered length, like new-cut lead and new-cut copper. His tail and fins were pink – a handsome cock-fish who had travelled across the Atlantic for love.

A Sunday Walk on Exmoor

Come with us this morning for a walk the children and I usually take on a Sunday.

Leaving the cottage gate we turn to the right up the steep stony track which the timber wagons during the past few rainy weeks have churned into twin muddy watercourses.

The track lies up the side of a hill, with a plantation of larch trees on one side and another kind of pine on the other. In both plantations foxes find dense cover among the bracken and brambles growing under the sapling trees.

Wild pigeons fly out of the larches and a buzzard is soaring in the cold north wind which for days has been sweeping across the clear bright sky.

It is warm between the plantations, but as we turn down a ride to the left which takes us round the crest of the hill we meet the wind with its icy cutting edge. Here the trees of a much older plantation are maimed or 'burned', as we say in Devon, by the winter winds which sweep down the valley from Exmoor, which we see, bleak and grey, before us as we walk on.

By this time our bodies are glowing with the walk, and the children run on ahead uttering their cries of the hunting game they are playing. The path leads down hill, past small beech trees rattling their brittle castanets of dead leaves in the wind.

We pass a trail of white hen's feathers and know that a fox has been raiding the hen-roost of a farmer in the valley below.

The best part of the walk now begins for the children. We climb under a wire-spanned fence and walk in a railway cutting where a single track is laid. We hurry along the cinder track with backward glances lest a train be coming, although we know none run here on Sunday.

Soon we come to the viaduct, lying beyond the cutting opening. We walk above the tops of spruce trees sinking away, and then see only the grass far below. The wind sighs in the iron-work of the parapet, and below the river looks cold and shallow.

Down by the edge of a pool a heron is standing. We know he has seen us by the way his head is anxiously held up.

Hullo, what has John found lying between the metals, apparently a drab bundle of dead leaves?

It has a long beak and slender legs: a woodcock, probably hit by a passing train. 'Can we eat it?' asks John. We decide to bury it and put a stone on the little grave in the wood beyond the viaduct.

Afterwards we take hands and run down a stony way between the trees and so to the valley where the river is running, its gravelly bed new-looking in places where spawning salmon have dug to lay their eggs.

Margaret is tired by this time, so she rides on my back. Windles and John run on looking for dead salmon which the otter may have caught and left on a stone under the bank somewhere.

We hear a water-ousel singing, and the deep croak of a raven passing over in the sky.

When we come home there is cider for dinner, a Sunday treat, and we toast each other before the blazing hearth.

Peal Leaping

The recent rain filled the springs of Exmoor, for the river has remained at 'running' level for several days. More salmon have come up to Stag's Head Weir. I watched them turning up against the strakes of white water.

They were not seriously jumping. They were exploring. They were feeling the weight of the water. So were the sea-trout, which were making half-serious attempts to jump-and-wriggle up the various cascades of their individual choice.

The water was not heavy enough for an ascent of the falls by any fish of more than two pounds' weight.

In very heavy water fish of all weights over a pound can swim up confidently at an angle of sixty degrees; but in lesser water they are afraid of being hurt against the stones below the sill.

I saw one sea-trout – otherwise an ordinary brown trout, which had wandered to the sea, grown big and fat quickly, and returned because his sexual desire was stimulated prematurely by good feeding – get up into the deep water of the mill-pool above.

He must have tested the way up in many attempts before my arrival, probably watched by that lean ragamuffin of a heron, for he came out of the water in a grand flying leap, at an angle of forty-five degrees.

I saw him wriggling into position between two mossy stones, a favourite resting-place of sea trout of his weight – about two pounds.

His tail curled against the moss. He gripped the rock with his paived fins. He waited there about half a minute, while the white water spirted from off his back. He would never get up, I thought . . . and then suddenly he sprang, to *grip* the hard descending mixture of air and water with scale and caudal fin, to bore into it with nose and eyes and gills and all the determined strength of life being urged forward.

For several seconds the trout hung there, quivering violently, vertical and sinuating, hardly moving. Its sea strength, now being spent so violently, was equal to the calm impersonal force of the water which had made and shaped its earlier life.

It gained an inch; it remained there, boring desperately upwards; then in a final drive it mounted to where bubbles were whirled into the lip of the sill. It shot over the edge into deeper water, making a ream or wavelet which immediately was smoothed and carried away behind it.

At the tail of the pool, belly hardly touching the gravel, the fish rested; surely life was pleasing, for it threw itself out of the water and fell back on its side with what seemed to be a deliberate splash.

Out of the Mouths of Babes . . .

For some years the rotting section of a beech tree lying by the river had reminded me that one day I must bring an iron bar and heave it into the water. Then it must be secured by wire rope to pegs driven into the gravel, otherwise the next spate would take it down into the Atlantic Ocean. The section was about nine feet long and two feet thick. For some reason it had been left when axemen and timber wagon crew had been working there about ten years before.

This last week I took a crowbar on shoulder and walked along the river bank determined to shift the log into the water. Dry-rot and other fungi had eaten most of its heart away. It was sodden on top, but the first heave rolled it over.

Immediately small daughter Margaret and I saw a number of interesting things.

A series of little tunnels lay exposed among pale roots of grasses in the hollow earth wherein the log had bedded itself.

Beside one gallery lay a ball of dry bitten grasses, the top of which had lifted away with the log. Within the ball lay two field mice, asleep. We could see their heads and forepaws; they appeared to be clasping one another in winter sleep. Then an eye opened and a head looked up. The eye blinked, a nose flaired, a whisker worked. Another eye, nose, and whisker peeked, twitched, and flitched. Two mouths opened simultaneously in a yawn.

Then, aware of the situation, the mice surveyed the ruin of their thatched roof, and the problem of earthquakes.

Meanwhile daughter Margaret gave a gasp, and, turning round, I saw a snake slowly uncoiling from a dry hole in the log. It was an adder, a thin, lanky sort of viper, the markings on its back much faded.

Out of the Mouths of Babes . . .

One of the mice hopped out of the grass ball. It was surprisingly fat for a mouse that slept so much.

The snake was trying to move along the earth – a very tired snake – for, after yawning, it paused and swayed its head drowsily. Its eye was half gummed up.

'Look!' cried Margaret. She pointed to a dark-brown nose poking out between dead beech leaves in a hole in the log. I touched it with a stick, and the ball fell on the grass. It lay there, unmoving. This was the third tenant of the log, a hedgehog.

Mentioning to Margaret that the hedgehog was probably very hungry, she said, 'Shall us give the snake to it, Dad? But what about the poor snake?'

Then I told her how snakes ate mice, and she said, 'Us mustn't let the nasty old snake eat a mouse; us must kill the snake. Oh, but what if the hedgehog eats the snake? We will kill the hedgehog, won't we, Dad?'

'What, kill that poor scared little thing, Margaret?' I asked.

'No, us'll kill nought, will us? Else God might kill us, mightn't He, Dad?'

Such philosophic argument being wearisome to my simple nature, we left log, mice, snake, and hedgehog to their own devices, and callously went home to eat roast mutton.

Life is Returning to the Moor

Here, in North Devon, on the high ground of the moor, we are open to the grey sky; the wind which for days and weeks has been veering from the cold north seems to have quenched all desire for life.

Below this high ridge valley after valley is sunken in mist. The sun behind clouds throws down shafts of light like the spokes of a wheel.

As the cloud moves slowly towards the south-east the sun wanly lights the withered ling and rushy grasses of the bog. The bells of the ling are bleached white, the stems are tough as though dead and the rising life in the whortleberry shoots is checked by the teeth of deer and wild ponies which wander here when no other life is moving.

But last night the west wind returned, bringing hope to the earth again.

A stone wall raised beside the track and bedded with peaty turfs marks a division of property. It seems strange that this moorland, incult for thousands of centuries, should be owned by anything except the wind and the sky.

A farmer's eye, however, sees it as rough pasture-land. Sheep made these tracks through the ling. Deer and ponies have trodden them wider. If there is a path anywhere, animals of all kinds will follow it, as will men. See, this greyish pellet of fur and broken bone tells that a fox prowls here. A hard life it must be for him in winter.

The storms have beaten and twisted the broad yellow grass blades from the dead tufts and driven them over the rough face of the moor. The children notice how they have lodged between the wires and posts of the fence on top of the wall. So neatly and regularly are the grasses laid in bunches that at first it looks as though a child, impelled by some fancy, has gone along and carefully placed them in position. The unseen child is the west wind.

We scramble under the low wire of the rack, as this deer fence is called, and continue our walk among rushes and grasses slightly less coarse. Now the reason for building a wall is plain; this is, or was, reclaimed ground.

As we walk on we see the first sign of life – black peaty earth moving as an invisible mole beneath clears out its gallery after the land-falls caused by the recent frost.

Before us lies a rounded mound of earth which the children climb in order to run down again with arms spread for flight. They utter wild bird-like cries.

For how many centuries has the ancient warrior been resting in his tumulus, about him the everlasting wind sighing in heather and rushes, while the dark rain clouds lifted from off the Atlantic and beat down upon this wild place? Did the wild man wish for burial here in order to perpetuate his spirit's freedom nearest the sky?

Maybe he is still here, though unseen, and the natural cries of the children which arose so blithely and thoughtlessly a moment ago are of his spirit.

Hill-top Meditations

Here on the hill-top the wind is sharp and keen; down there the winter fields lie under the smoke of the Black Country. Factory chimneys pour their poison at the sky – the poison that is of the sun's power of olden time, transmuted into living leaf and branch and trunk, and now so woefully misused by men.

'Woefully misused?' asks someone; 'it's time that pseudo-philosophical attitude about coal, machinery, and industrial civilisation was abandoned. You drive a car, and enjoy its speed; you are of modern life, enjoying its conveniences – so why this attitude because smoke hangs over the factories where your car, and the other things you use and approve, are produced? Why not accept these things calmly, as inevitable and interesting phenomena of human, or, if you prefer it, cosmic activity? Why attitudinise yourself to part of the means whereby scissors, silk, ploughs, cotton thread, are made?'

The voice continued: 'I agree that what we saw down there by the allotments outside the town was deplorable; but everywhere in the world will be found irritable, frustrated men ill-treating small children. I agree that it is dreadful to hear a pale, weedy father swearing in that cold, obscene way before thrashing his pale, weedy little boy, who sobs with pain and despair.

'Are the smoke, the mill, the polluted river, the cold sweating cobble stones, the morning bray of the factory "blower", the life-slavery, alone responsible? I can show you men who have always lived here who are kind, jolly and full of zest. But look at that colour!'

We were standing by the millstone-grit quarries of Teg's Nose, a thousand feet above the fields, towns, and factory chimneys small and remote as though drowned under a ghostly sea.

Down there the air was damp and still; up here the wind blew hard and steady, with a cutting-edge of glass. It scooped tears from our eyes.

A solitary pipit fluttered into the wind, made no headway, and turning, was immediately thrown out of sight.

The sun sinking upon the iodine-brown smoke-scape was an imperfect shield against death, a shield forged in ill-shape by the crude efforts of Man who abused the ancient solar power in coal, wasting its virtue, poisoning its sky. But the new forge is being built; man can make of life, which is the sun, what he will.

The Mystery of the Orange Ship

Like yellow beads they lay along the tide-line, among cast-up bottles, seaweed, crab-shells, feathers of gulls and curlews, branches and roots of trees, broken crab-pots, and, curiously, six straw palliasses or mattresses. The line of jetsam lay at the foot of the sandhills, thrown there by the last waves of the high spring tide driven further inland by the south-west gale.

Among the tangle and litter hundreds of oranges were lying, bright spots of colour in the greyness of the winter's day.

When the children saw them they ran forward to gather them. Having pushed one into each trouser pocket, John and Windles began to stuff their jerseys with them. Margaret held two in her hands, while vainly trying to conceal another in the pocket of her skirt which her mother had sewn there for a handkerchief. Once again she learned that it was much better to be a boy. She returned slowly. 'I've only got three,' she said, near to tears.

When one had been peeled for her and she saw it was rotted by the salt water she brightened; and when, further, she saw it could be used as a ball to roll down the wet sands she gave a cry and ran away to tell the boys to roll all the oranges down the sand.

'Look, John; you throw one up in the air and try and hit it with another one, like this. Look, John! Watch, John!'

'No; if you kick it hard it busts; you play this way, Win.'

'All right; only when I pass to you, you must pass it back, like football, see? Only don't keep the ball too long. Pass! Come on, pass! John, will you obey me? Oh, you're no good.'

Windles walked away by himself.

'Windles, let's throw some down towards those gulls, and see if they fly up, or if they will know it is only an orange. Now then, both together.'

The gulls merely walked away, regarding us with watchful suspicion.

'Daddy, can't we sell them? People won't know they be bad, they don't look bad, do'm?'

'Was there a wreck, do you think, Dad? John, you fool, don't throw that at Margaret. I'll chuck one at you, and hard, if you do!'

'I don't care!'

We began to throw them hard on the sand, to burst them. Soon we were weary of oranges. Tens of thousands lay along the tideline. One only had been nibbled by a rat, who appeared to have found it uneatable.

By their size and shape they looked to be Florida oranges. Had the cargo boat been wrecked? How had they been packed – loose, or in crates? For if they had been loose, then surely the boat had foundered. And those straw mattresses, were they from the boat, too?

One could see that the balance of Nature had been disturbed by the sight of so many oranges, and to even things up the children were pushed over all together in a heap of seaweed.

They picked themselves up and began to bombard their father, a common enemy for the moment, while the gulls, birds without any sense of fun, living all their lives in competition for food, huddled immobile on the sands below, wondering what it was all about.

Pigeons Come to Breakfast

By the window at which I am sitting there comes periodically the noise of rushing wind, as wild pigeons fly over the house and dive to the lawn below.

Their spread wings are blue-grey against the dull green of the grass. They settle and walk slowly about searching for acorns which, during the winter rains, have sunk into the grass.

During the autumn the oaks at the edge of the lawn dropped scores of thousands of their hard yellow seeds, and the pigeons came in hundreds, picking them up and gulping them until they were double their size.

This is no exaggeration; some birds within a few minutes must have doubled their weight by swallowing so many acorns. They walked heavily, waddling along, their breast feathers puffed out, their heads held low, their crops touching the ground.

Even so, some birds gorged until they could not close their beaks, but sat about in the grass waiting for the acorns to settle down.

Most of the pigeons were visitors from the great forests of Norway, crossing the sea to the rich feeding of East Anglia when the first icicles hung by the cascades of their wooded valley.

Soon they will be returning across the North Sea, fat with English acorns, to make their raft-like nests – mere platforms of twigs – in the fir-trees, and lay their two eggs.

Now the farmers in this country have organised their local pigeon shoots, to which, usually, anyone who owns or can borrow a gun is made welcome. For the wild pigeons, or ring doves as they are sometimes called, are almost what is called vermin. That is to say, they eat what man requires for himself.

A few weeks ago I saw from this same window a cat stalking the birds feeding under the oaks. The cat knew their greed for acorns, and waited until a visiting flock had gorged itself.

Then it ran forward. Most of the birds flew up, clapping wings overhead to give the alarm. Three birds, however, were unable to arise. They waddled through the grass, flapping their wings, but held down by their loads of acorns. The cat caught one easily.

I ran downstairs and into the garden, but by the time I got there the bird was dead and partly eaten. There were forty-seven acorns in its crop – large acorns, too.

I know a scrub oak plantation in North Devon which is called Dovey Brake, for all the trees were planted from acorns which the owner had taken from shot pigeons. And one day, while standing on a hill near a cattle shippen, or shed, with a corrugated iron roof, I was amazed to hear a loud rattle on the roof and to see what turned out to be acorns bounding off.

I looked about me and was mystified for several minutes until the breast feather of a pigeon floating down in the still air told me that a peregrine falcon must have struck a bird high in the air, and the shock of impact had broken open its crop.

The Country Awakes from its Winter Sleep

Dimly aware that the children were awake very early, for it was still dark, I looked at the luminous hands of my wristlet watch. Half-past six. A strange pallor was in the room, and it was cold. Then I realised that the children's voices were not coming from the night nursery, but from somewhere below.

They were on the lawn by the yew tree, which was white like the rest of the earth. They were pelting one another with handfuls of snow, which was too fine and dry to bind.

Shouting to them to put on their coats, and reminding them of colds, pneumonia, and other grown-up fear-manifestations, I crept into bed again and tried to sleep. But soon the door was opening, and the *clup-clup* of rubber boots on the beechwood floor.

'Dad, dad, wake up. Look! Wake up, lazy bones! Look, snow! Look, isn't it lovely!'

The happy voice drew a grunt from me. I turned over, huddled the blankets closer and prepared to go to sleep again. But Margaret tugged at the blankets. I sat up. John had come silently, as usual, into the room. They were tousle-headed but dressed in their outdoor clothes. On my elbow I looked out of the leaded casement window and saw the trees and cottages and hedges outside white and glistening, the sky blue, and the sun shining. It was seven-thirty.

Reluctantly I agreed to get dressed. Outside it was a bright new world, but I found myself wishing it were the Tyrol, deep snow, where I could bind on my skis and set off with friends in the morning.

Here the snow was a mere two inches deep. In the Deer Park it was already scored by the tracks of sheep, sets of parallel lines wandering as though aimlessly in the white. There they were, a flock of small black sheep which had come down from the hills to the valley.

The water of the river looked strange, shadowed darkly green, for the sun was still below the tops of the spruces on the eastern hillside. Looking down, one felt oneself to be cold and in shadow; but looking up, and without moving, one was of a world of shining whiteness and blue sky. A cold world, too, with the wind in the north, so we set off to run over the white grass. The children scooped up handfuls of snow and threw it over their heads, sparkling in the sun.

We found the footprints of a heron, where it had walked beside the water. And the otter had scratched the snow by the anthill, where it always 'touches' when travelling upriver. A hare had gone limping towards the trees, pheasants had sipped by the shallows, jackdaws walked around the dead salmon-kelt thrown on the grass. Now the fish, which after spawning last December had died of fungus disease and exhaustion, was hidden by snow. Everything was white – a new shining world.

'Look,' said John, letting go my hand and stopping. He bent over a mound of fresh brown earth, with no trace of snow – a mole had just made a new tunnel.

The old world was beginning to return already.

The Love Song of the Curlew

The other day I went to visit friends in a house which faces the water-front of Appledore in North Devon. This pleasant fishing village lies across the estuary of the River Torridge, and consists of a cluster of cottages around a low hill grown with trees.

On going to bed, I saw a sight that would have made that fine artist Mr C R W Nevinson sit up all night to paint it.

The tide was lapsing silently; the reflections of the quay lamps shimmered and shook in gold on the water. Over the hill a small moon rode in the pale Atlantic vapours, diffusing moonshine among the quavering water-images of the Appledore lights.

Later, lying in bed and watching the lights framed in the open window, I heard the cries of wading birds arising from the tide-line on sandbank and gravel-ridge. So quiet were air and water that the piping and trilling of individual birds were carried from the estuary mouth, two miles to the west.

All these cries were frail and musical, but the most thrilling came from the curlews – lovely eye-lashes of sound, one falling after another delicately, lyrically, descending in scale until the last of the song falls like water-drops.

This is clumsy description, as all must be that attempts to render song into words.

The curlew's love cry in spring is the most beautiful sky-sound of the West Country. It is pure poetry; it is passion that is the highest joy of living – true love.

Very soon the curlews will be leaving the estuary shores and flying to the moors, where, among rushes and red cotton-grass of the bogs, they will make their nests and lay their large eggs blotched and coloured as the ground around them.

After the young are hatched, the song becomes more tender;

time after time the father bird flies up and descends slowly to his mate and little ones, his hooped wings downheld, song dropping from his long, curved beak. Gravely and slowly he alights; his wings upheld are slowly folded, while the chicks run to him and his mate feeds her singer – the perfect family, the perfect love.

A Message of Hope from the West

This morning I saw the spring. I was sitting in a chair on the path in front of a lime-washed cottage, while the sun shone hotly on the pear-tree behind.

For days and weeks and months the tree-tops seen through the window had swayed to the mindless music of the north wind, and there was no hope on the earth. Nothing grew; life was suspended.

Then, suddenly, this morning the cream-coloured distempered walls of the cottage interior were glowing with light, a bumblebee was buzzing under the thatch, and the cry of a bird with black cap and white cheeks in the lichened branches of the apple trees was like the gay ringing of a little bell.

It is no fancy or anthropomorphical sentimentality to say that Hope was in the valley. Hope was there, an intangible force in the sunlight, a creative impulse.

Daffodils which had been drooping on the borders lifted up yellow heads to their golden god. During the winds and rains they had waited, having drawn life from their bulbs, from which the stored sunlight had all been taken. There was nothing more to do. But with the true shining of the sun the green stalks and leaves glistened with renewed hope, and slowly their heads turned in beauty to the heavenly fire.

The mindless winds had gone, and there was a delicious warm silence in the valley. Far away the cawing of rooks told that they, too, were rejoicing in the new lease of life.

In a few days spring will be rushing on the west wind over Devon and the West, the willow wren and the chiffchaff will be here, smouldering wallflowers will flame in dark brown beauty, aubretia on the borders will mass blue flowers for our morning delight.

A Message of Hope from the West

Those plashes in the lane will be dry, the ruts under the limes, desolate daily sight for many months as one walked the same way in all weathers, will be trodden out, and grass will spring there again.

And what was that? A dark flick on the wall beside me, where many hand-forged nails, to which in olden time pear-branches were fixed, are rusting in the plaster.

Strange: I thought I saw something move there. Keep still and watch.

Hullo, there it is again. A lizard! So that's where he has been sleeping all the winter, is it? In the dry crack between plaster and cob-wall. And only last week I was thinking of cementing up those places where the plaster has cracked and gaped.

So with the lizard and I warming winter out of ourselves, among flowers and bees, and to the ringing of avian bells, I end this message of hope from the West Country.

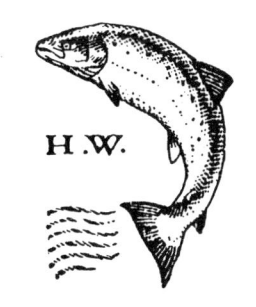